Be the Cat

Be the Cat

SECRETS OF THE NATURAL CAT OWNER

Steve Duno

For my favourite cat owner! Happy Birthday! 7.10.10 love mom

🌳 **STERLING**

New York / London
www.sterlingpublishing.com

STERLING and the distinctive Sterling logo are registered trademarks of
Sterling Publishing Co., Inc.

Library of Congress Cataloging-in-Publication Data

Duno, Steve.
    Be the cat: secrets of the natural cat owner / Steve Duno.
        p. cm.
    Includes index.
    ISBN 978-1-4027-5278-0
        1. Cat owners—Psychology. 2. Cats—Psychological aspects.
    3. Human-animal relationships. I. Title.

SF442.86.D86 2008
636.8—dc22

                                  2008001474

10 9 8 7 6 5 4 3 2 1

Published by Sterling Publishing Co., Inc.
387 Park Avenue South, New York, NY 10016
© 2008 by Steve Duno
Distributed in Canada by Sterling Publishing
c/o Canadian Manda Group, 165 Dufferin Street
Toronto, Ontario, Canada M6K 3H6
Distributed in the United Kingdom by GMC Distribution Services
Castle Place, 166 High Street, Lewes, East Sussex, England BN7 1XU
Distributed in Australia by Capricorn Link (Australia) Pty. Ltd.
P.O. Box 704, Windsor, NSW 2756, Australia

Manufactured in the United States of America
All rights reserved

Sterling ISBN 978-1-4027-5278-0

For information about custom editions, special sales, premium and
corporate purchases, please contact Sterling Special Sales Department
at 800-805-5489 or specialsales@sterlingpublishing.com.

Contents

PART ONE

From Granaries to Vanities:

The Changing Cat/Owner Dynamic

With the gratitude of the first farmers nearly ten thousand years ago, the rapport between cats and humans began. No one knows precisely where or when this occurred, though the remains of a cat found in the 9500-year-old grave of a Cypriot citizen appears to have been purposely placed there, indicating ownership of and affection for the feline proto-pet. As the isle of Cyprus had no cat species native to it, it seems that they were intentionally introduced to the atoll for a specific reason.

About the same time of the Cypriot burial, the collection and storage of wild grains and seeds began. Soon wild plants were cultivated, ensuring a steady supply of food through hard times. The ensuing agricultural revolution allowed permanent towns and cities to form for the first time in human history; populations grew, and with them, culture.

These first farmers suffered crop loss to mice and rats, which, upon discovering such vast stores of grain in one place, must have thought they had found easy street. But their free ride wouldn't last long. As the grain was to rodents, so would the rodents soon be to cats.

The African wild cat, or *Felis sylvestris lybica*, was no dummy. Originally native to the African continent, it is acknowledged to be the direct ancestor of today's domestic cat, *Felis sylvestris catus* (though taxonomists still aren't yet in full agreement on this scientific name). These small wild cats quickly became attracted to the human grain stores, not for the grain itself, but for an easy meal of rodents feeding on the grain. Cats lack taste buds for sweet, and as such have no desire to eat grain-based foods; farmers therefore had no worry over crop loss to cats (unlike poochy, who will eat anything).

A mutual relationship began; cats kept thieving rodents at bay, while the farmers' grain, acting as a rodent lure, guaranteed a steady supply of food for the clever wild cats. The cats also knew that predators perhaps hungry for a bit of cat tended to avoid human towns, making us even more useful.

Over time these felines became desensitized to the presence of people. Though the word "pet" might not have initially applied, the clean and helpful cats soon became an accepted part of life for early agricultural societies.

The Egyptians domesticated, revered and even deified the cat, whose mummified bodies were often buried with great honor. In fact, Egyptian records indicate that a law existed calling for the death penalty for anyone found guilty of killing a cat. Talk about animal rights!

Plagued by onboard rats, early sailors made a point of keeping a few cats aboard to protect stores of food. These seagoing cats soon found their way to ports of call in Europe, Asia, and all parts of the known world. Like humans, domesticated cats spread from their African beginnings to all parts, becoming a useful partner and exotic friend.

Kitty Ups and Downs

Good times for European cats unfortunately came to a grinding halt during the Middle Ages, when they somehow became *catus non gratis*, as it were. Their mystique became inextricably associated with devil worship; labeled servants of Satan, they were condemned indiscriminately by the Church in Europe. For hundreds of years millions of cats suffered persecution, torture and death, causing their numbers to crash.

Ironically, the wholesale kill-off of cats in Europe played a role in the epidemic spread of the bubonic plague, a killer disease spread by infected fleas on the backs of rats, whose numbers soared in part because of the anti-cat crusade. Interestingly, cat persecutions occurred largely in urban areas; rural cats stood a better chance of escaping harassment. Deaths from the plague reflected this; most victims died in the crowded cat-free cities and not the countryside.

With the coming of the Renaissance, religious extremism eased, and with it the persecution of cats. Henry III of France, Nostradamus, Newton, da Vinci —all found the company of cats captivating. Slowly the number of breeds increased and spread throughout Europe, Asia, and the Americas, until the domestic feline became an accepted fixture around the globe. Wherever there was the storage of foodstuffs, cats would be there to control the vermin and captivate their providers.

The Shifting Cat/Owner Dynamic

As we entered the Industrial Age, the cat's elegant camaraderie, ease of care and wily ways began to win over millions of pet fans living in suburbs and cities. The job of "vermin police" became less crucial due to advances in sanitation, and to the regionalization and automation of farming. No longer an essential element of farm life, adaptable felines won their way into the homes and apartments of people whose sole desire was for pet companionship.

Easier to care for than the more sociable, needy dog, they have eventually overtaken their canine cousins in popularity. In the United States, for example, the eighty million cats outnumber dogs by nearly twenty million. To put that into perspective, U.S. children under the age of eighteen number a hair under eighty million, making cats more popular than kids!

For millennia, domesticated cats lived life without much human help; so long as there was a plentiful supply of rodents and a warm, dry place to sleep, they were happy. Even when rural populations began to feed and house their felines, it was understood that they would have unrestricted access to the outdoors, where their natural instinct to hunt could be satisfied. With human and cat population densities low and natural cat predators scarce, being outside all day posed little threat to their safety. Even today, in certain rural areas, many cats come and go as they please with little threat to their well-being.

The inexorable change from rural ratter to urban/suburban home companion has changed much about the way cats live. Instead of acres of farmland outside the front door, we now have streets and highways, densely populated asphalt-covered metropolises, skyscrapers, fast cars, and a dizzying array of outdoor hazards that even the adaptable cat cannot easily conform to.

But many cat aficionados, perhaps lulled by the feline's furtive ways and physical prowess, disregard the dangers and allow their pets unsupervised access to today's chaotic outdoors. Even though conditions have changed, many owners have not; they still think family felines can roam free without risk.

The rural cat owner of yesterday had more than low population density on his or her side. Able to watch their cats interacting with their environment in an instinctive, unaffected way, those owners came to understand natural cat behavior on an intimate level, perhaps more so than many owners today whose cats often take on the role of surrogate child. Rural owners saw true stalking behavior, watched territorial displays with other cats, observed mating rituals, and understood how cats interacted with their environment. And they were present more often than cat owners today, whose 9-to-5 lifestyles allow them less time to observe and interact.

The "Natural" versus the "Confused" Owner

Cats are easier to own than dogs, who because of their social nature and need for direction require owners to spend blocks of time teaching, training, and socializing. Dogs need the right conditioning and guidance; without it they invariably make poor pets. Cats need less direction from us; they quickly become litter box trained, and have good hygiene skills and a more manageable demeanor than the average new dog. Simply providing the right environment, teaching some rudimentary boundary training and pointing out the location of the litter box, and cats are as close to "auto pilot" as a pet can get.

Nevertheless, today's cat owners still experience behavioral problems with their pets. From destructive behavior, eating disorders or excessive vocalizations to roaming, biting, scratching or even outright aggressive behavior, behavioral problems with cats abound. Cats can also suffer from a multitude of preventable health issues directly related to diet, environment or quality of care. Perhaps cat ownership isn't so easy after all.

Let's get right to it; some cat owners are just naturally *better* at it than others. By adopting a more intuitive approach to cat ownership and developing what I call *effective feline empathy*, these "natural-born" owners head behavioral and physiological problems off at the pass, ensuring that life for their household kitties will be as good as it gets. Effective cat owners, rather than attempting to turn their cats into proxy humans, instead *turn themselves into proxy cats*. Their abiding theme remains *"be the cat."* They sense and interpret their environments with near catlike perception, the calling card of the natural cat owner and a key factor in achieving the goal of a happy pet.

The natural cat owner enters a calm, attentive place from which he or she has entry into a cat's world. He or she *belongs*, like a tribal elder who has a better grasp on his or her own culture than does an anthropologist sent from another civilization to study and interpret. The natural owner anticipates a cat's reactions and senses when something is amiss—often from just a glance, a vocalization, or a faintly atypical response. The "natural" feels a rapport, and sees things from the inside looking out.

The "confused" owner, despite an abiding love for cats, doesn't quite get it. He or she hasn't yet developed the ability to experience things from a cat's perspective, and hasn't figured out just what it takes to make a cat happy and fulfilled. He or she will over- or under-stimulate, abruptly alter home conditions, or miss subtle signs of illness or impending misbehavior. He or she hasn't yet learned to *"be the cat."*

Not everyone can claim to be a natural-born cat person. Many well-meaning "newbie" owners haven't the wisdom of more experienced cat fans, particularly with regard to basic feline needs and instincts. For instance, new owners often know little about a cat's constraints as a social creature, and may mistakenly attempt to place their pets into intense social situations more suitable to a dog or person. New owners might also not be aware of just how fond cats are of the status quo, and how hard it can be for a cat to adapt to a new situation such as a move, a new baby, or even a home remodel.

Old-school cat aficionados make mistakes too. Accustomed to letting their cats outdoors, they often fail to take into consideration the effects of urbanization, and of the burgeoning cat population. In an attempt to mirror the "good old days," they can expose their cats to the perils of neighborhood sprawl. Another "old-school" flaw is the hesitance of many to take cats in to a qualified veterinarian for a yearly preventive health care exam. Even among many conscientious cat lovers, the trend is often to wait until a cat shows obvious signs of illness before seeking medical help. Cat owners also seem less apt to get their pets the proper important vaccinations. Those who take this attitude are not "natural" cat owners.

Confused cat owners often don't realize how inquisitive cats really are. Being among the world's best hunters, the cat has an intimate connection with her environment, and a daily need for sensory stimulation. Unlike wild counterparts who lead dynamic, stimulating lives, most domestic cats are denied this sensory outlet, becoming bored and stressed in the process, and living life like a zoo cat from the 1950s. Natural cat owners make sure to provide their pets with plenty of environmental and behavioral stimulation, or "enrichment," to appeal to the cat's predatory need to investigate and hunt. Owners who deny their cats enrichment set the stage for all manner of behavioral problems.

Cats are easy to maintain but sometimes challenging to adapt to new conditions. If something new appears in the cat's life, be it a different litter box, a new kitten or an owner's new spouse, the cat will be slow to adapt, and can evidence bad behaviors as a result. Natural cat owners instinctively keep the living environment as stable as possible; when change needs to occur it is introduced gradually, with little pomp. Changes in food, litter, lighting—even the type of carpet cleaner you use—all these can impact your cat's mood and behavior. Natural cat owners bring change on gradually and positively, with little spectacle;

confused owners often drop bombs on their cats and then are surprised when unexpected behaviors occur.

Natural owners are also good at identifying individual cats' personalities, and then using that subjective knowledge in their everyday interactions. For example, in a two-cat home, one cat might be shy and averse to touch, while the other loves to mix it up and get carried and petted. The natural owner knows to respond to each cat accordingly; the shy cat is allowed to set its own "rules of engagement," while the more confident pet's love of interaction is encouraged, not only to satisfy it, but also as a means to gradually lure the other cat in petting/handling situations. In an effort to desensitize the shy cat, a confused owner might over-handle her, with the end result being a decreased desire for touch.

The goal of this book is to identify the qualities inherent to "natural" cat owners, and then present them to you in an understandable, easy-to-implement manner. I want you to in effect *"be the cat,"* to sense things from the inside and know intuitively what your cat needs, why she behaves the way she does, and how to create the optimal environment for her to be happy and problem-free.

I'm going to show you how to become a natural cat owner by sharing with you what I call the *Secrets*, principles I believe every natural cat owner intuitively understands and applies to the relationship with his or her cat. From selection, environment and education to health, enrichment and the importance of consistency, I'll take you through all seven, and explain how to integrate them all into your cat's world. I'll teach you how to be a "natural," and how to deepen your cat/owner connection, so that, in time, you too can "be the cat." In effect you will learn to empathize with the feline condition, making the job of an owner much easier and more fulfilling. So without further ado, let's begin!

Secrets of the Natural Cat Owner

The "Secrets" aren't secretive at all, at least not to natural cat owners. Rather, they simply relate to cats in a relaxed, sympathetic manner, and understand intuitively what to do, how to teach, what limits to set. No one is actually keeping secrets; rather, the information has been lost over the years, by owners more concerned with their cats' appearances than in their behavior.

In Part Two I re-establish forgotten knowledge, reintroduce poise to the partnership, and give you a chance to understand what it really means to be an effective member of one of history's most successful collaborations.

This is not a tribute to days gone by. On the contrary, the past contained heartless, often cruel treatment of cats. *Be the Cat* combines yesterday's empathies with today's sympathies, creating a blend of methodologies which teaches, protects, and normalizes.

Before you begin, pet your cat. Watch and listen to her, and notice how she relates to you. Moreover, try to sense things yourself, and guess at what she is thinking. Begin to become aware in a feline way.

SECRET ONE:
Know Your Cat

Using Species, Breed, History, and Personality to Your Advantage

The natural cat owner gets off on the right foot by learning as much as possible about his or her cat's unique physiology, breed, history and personality. By understanding what your cat's innate predispositions are, you'll get a huge head start on nurturing the ideal relationship. And for those in the market for a new cat, knowing which cat will best fit into your lifestyle is also a crucial component in guaranteeing a successful, satisfying pet/owner team.

Feline Physiology

Being aware of the unique physiology of your cat will help you understand her needs and behavior, so let's take a quick look. The domestic cat is one of the smallest felines; only the Black-footed cat of South Africa and the Oncilla and Kodkod of South America appear smaller.

Averaging from five to fifteen pounds and eight to ten inches in height, the domestic cat evolved as a warm-weather predator with uncanny athletic abilities and unparalleled predatory instincts. True (or obligate) carnivores, cats are nocturnal by nature, but readily adapt to daytime activity when in our care. Cats are fast and strong for their size, with explosive, "fast-twitch" muscular power meant to be used in bursts of speed, to catch equally quick prey. Unlike dogs, they do not have great stamina, and cannot exert themselves for long periods.

Your cat's senses control how she relates to you and her environment. They rule her ability to interpret, analyze and communicate, so let's look at them quickly, to better understand where she is coming from:

Sight
Cats are renowned for their specialized vision, especially under low-light conditions. The domestic cat and other small cats have a slitted iris, which can dramatically reduce the amount of available light and improve depth-of-field. (Curiously, big cats such as the lion and tiger have rounded pupils, much like our own.) A reflective coating on the cat's retina known as the *tapetum lucidum* amplifies the amount of light available during low-light conditions, allowing felines to hunt in near pitch-black conditions. They have a slightly wider field of vision than humans, but see colors poorly. Cats notice movement more acutely than do we, but do not recognize stationary objects quite as well. Consequently, prey animals, if not close to an escape route, stand the best chance of survival by keeping as still as possible.

Hearing
Your cat's hearing is keener than your own. She can perceive much higher frequency sounds, allowing her to home in on the high-pitched noises uttered by small, delectable rodents and birds. The cat's large ears can be rotated 180 degrees, allowing her to funnel sound and accurately locate prey. The feline inner ear, with three semi-circular canals arranged ninety degrees to each other, controls your cat's amazing ability to determine spatial location in three dimensions. These, along with motion-sensing hair called *cilias,* help the cat develop a full sense of location, speed, motion and direction.

Smell
Your cat's sense of smell, though not as keen as a dog's, is much sharper than your own. Designed not only to locate prey but to detect predators and competitors, the feline nose deftly identifies the scent markings of

other cats, helping to avoid territorial disputes. In addition to the cat's keen nose, she has two specialized organs in her palate called *Jacobson's organs*, which allow her to detect specialized scents such as pheromones. If you have ever seen a cat curl back her lips into a sort of odd grimace while sucking air in and out of her mouth, you have watched her use these organs.

Taste

Your cat's taste buds are not as developed as those of humans or dogs. She cannot effectively taste sweet or salty, but can sense bitter and sour, and may be able to taste the presence of meat-based amino acids, something we cannot do. Suffice it to say her sense of taste is developed enough for her to distinguish between food types.

Touch

Your cat has a highly developed sense of touch. Her paw pads are quite sensitive to temperature and surface irregularities, and are regularly used to test and probe. Most of us have had a cat gently touch us with a paw; it's not only a sign of affection but an examination of your skin, body heat, and overall "feel." Cats use this sensory tactic much more than dogs.

In addition to sensitive pads, your cat has whiskers on her face, chin, eyes, legs, and other locations. Buried deep into the skin, they communicate to nerve cells much about the cat's environment. Often used in low-light conditions to tell a cat about spatial constraints, whiskers can also inform a cat about air currents, and even the presence of miniscule temperature changes caused by the approach of prey or predator.

Breed

Not all cats are created equal. As similar as cats are in appearance and basic behavior, it's a mistake to assume they don't each possess unique characteristics, or that some might have a bigger aesthetic impact on us than others. Though not as varied in appearance and behavior as dogs,

the over forty breeds of cats (and the innumerable mixed breed variations) present a wide variety of size, behavior, and personality from
which to choose. Anyone with a Siamese knows how gregarious and
vocal they can be, in comparison to, say, the larger, quieter, more
reserved Persian. Owners of American Shorthairs are as familiar with
the personalities of their amiable, robust pets as Chartreux owners are
of their massive cats' mild nature and tiny voice. Breed, therefore does
play a large role in defining not only a cat's appearance, but its base
behavior as well.

A basic difference between breeds is coat length. Curiously, longhaired cats tend to be a bit more reserved than their shorthaired
counterparts. Though certainly not a hard, fast rule, it is a fairly reliable
indicator of basic personality. Shorthaired breeds such as the Siamese,
Abyssinian, American Shorthair and others tend to be active and
outgoing, while longhaired breeds such as the Persian, Norwegian
Forest Cat and Ragdoll lean toward the sweet, shy side. If your cat is a
shorthaired breed or breed mix, look for her to have a somewhat greater
tolerance of strangers and activity than a longhaired breed, who might
take a bit longer to accept new people or unpredictable situations.

Sample Breed Profiles

To give you an idea of just how the breeds differ physically and behaviorally, I'm including five cat breed profiles here for your perusal. These
five breeds are some of the most common seen today:

The Abyssinian

The sleek, lithe Abyssinian is a muscular, elegant animal of medium
size, with a short, dense coat resembling that of a wild rabbit's pelt.
Individual hairs are uniquely colored, with a light portion at the base, a
coppery section in the middle, and a dark portion at the tip, giving it the
look of a tiny mountain lion. The Abyssinian's head is a rounded wedge,
topped by large, pointed, alert ears. Its large, expressive, almond-shaped
eyes can be green, hazel, or yellow. The Abyssinian's slender body, thin

legs and tapered tail give it a sinewy bearing. This breed's close resemblance to the mummified remains of cats found in ancient Egyptian tombs could point to truly archaic beginnings. The country of Ethiopia, formerly known as Abyssinia, is thought to be the first place that Europeans came into contact with the breed, during a war with the British in the 1860s. Others believe the Abyssinian to be a creation of selective breeding techniques in nineteenth-century Britain, in which British Shorthairs with ticked coats were interbred until the present-day look was achieved.

The Abyssinian is an active, intelligent, graceful cat, with a curious nature. Not content to rest placidly all day, she prefers regular interaction with her owner or another cat. An athletic breed, she is just as likely to be found atop your refrigerator or kitchen cupboard as anywhere else. The Abyssinian can show caution around newcomers, and won't enjoy roughhousing.

The owner of an Abyssinian must provide the cat with lots of love and attention. Highly intelligent, these cats need regular mental stimulation to remain healthy and happy. Raising an Abyssinian with another of the same age can often help both cats cope effectively with an absent working owner.

American Shorthair

A solid, strong cat, the American Shorthair's well-muscled body, rounded face, erect ears, and sturdy, long legs give it a robust, athletic look. Its short, dense coat comes in over eighty different color variations, with classic tabby, solid, and shaded or silver patterns being the most popular. The American Shorthair's rounded, lively eyes have a slight slant to them.

It is said that the descendants of today's American Shorthair came across with the pilgrims on the *Mayflower* in 1620. These and subsequent European settlers sailing to America in the seventeenth century brought with them their faithful hunting cats, primarily to help keep on-board rodent populations down to a minimum. These pioneering shorthaired cats were selectively bred over the centuries, slowly evolving into the uniquely American breed we know and love today.

A friendly, intelligent, sociable cat, the American Shorthair bonds quickly to all members of the family, and adapts well to nearly any environment. Though even-tempered, sociable, and sweet, this breed's working heritage reflects its present-day hunting skills, which remain unparalleled among domestic cats. Though appreciative of human companionship, the American Shorthair handles well being left home on its own while the owner is at work. A curious cat, most of this breed will show little fear or timidity when faced with new circumstances.

The American Shorthair will adapt well to nearly any environment, provided it is treated with respect by all members of the family. American Shorthairs should have a ready supply of teaser toys, stuffed mice, and wind-up or battery-operated toys on hand, to satisfy their stalking instincts, which are higher than the average cat. Also consider purchasing a carpeted, multi-tiered "kitty condo," to reduce this breed's exploratory instincts.

British Shorthair

A large, stocky cat with a massive head, thick neck, powerful legs and a short, wide tail, the British Shorthair sports a permanent, "Cheshire Cat" smile on its face, due to the unique shape of its whisker pads. Muscular, with a broad chest, this breed can weigh upwards of twelve to sixteen pounds, with males slightly heavier than the females. The British Shorthair's eyes are round and wide-set, with copper being their most common color. The ears, too, are wide-set atop the rounded head.

This breed's short, luxurious coat comes in many color variations, with blue being the most common. A British Shorthair of blue coloration can sometimes be mistaken for a Chartreuse, a French breed of similar build and color, but with a sharper muzzle and less stocky proportions.

The original British street cat, the British Shorthair has existed for centuries, and is said to be descended from ratter cats brought to the

British Isles by Roman occupation armies. Famed British cat fancier Harrison Weir helped solidify the breed in the late nineteenth century, allowing it to become the most successful show cat of that period, until eclipsed by the Persian in the early twentieth century.

Loving, tolerant, and intelligent, the British Shorthair is a quiet cat that develops strong attachments to its owners. An athlete and skilled hunter, this breed is often the first choice of Hollywood cat trainers, due to its aptitude for learning tricks and other new behaviors. Initially reserved toward strangers, it warms up quickly, and will get along perfectly with well-mannered children and dogs. Adaptable and undemanding, the British Shorthair is an inquisitive pet, and will love to stare out through the curtains to see what's happening at the local bird feeder.

This breed's tolerant, laid-back, accepting nature makes it an ideal pet for most homes. The owner of a British Shorthair will find it able to adapt to nearly any situation, even to interacting with children and dogs, provided they behave politely. The breed's short, plush coat will require a quick brushing only once or twice each week. Though short in length, the British Shorthair's coat is highly protective and insular, making it necessary for owners in hot climates to keep the indoor temperature at a reasonable level. Because of the breed's high intelligence, be sure to provide it with plenty of mental stimulation in the form of toys, a kitty condo, or a bird feeder outside a secured window.

Norwegian Forest Cat

Powerfully built, a fully mature Norwegian Forest Cat can weigh upwards of twenty pounds. A handsome animal, this breed has a full chest and strong rear legs slightly longer than the fronts. Its head is rounded, with a triangular face. The Norwegian Forest Cat's eyes are almond-shaped, and normally greenish-gold in color. The long, thick undercoat is topped with a water-resistant outer coat, allowing this breed to weather the coldest of climates. The tufted ears, full mane, and bushy tail help give this cat its Lynx-like appearance. Most colors and patterns are available, with brown tabby being the most popular.

An ancient breed mentioned in Norse mythology, the Norwegian Forest Cat lived as a farm cat for centuries before being discovered by cat enthusiasts in the early twentieth century. The cold conditions under which it developed helped create this breed's large body and plush coat, both of which are vital to survival in arctic conditions.

Intelligent and athletic, the Norwegian Forest Cat can be initially reserved around strangers, but always shows great affection for its family. A fine hunter, it excels at leaping and climbing. Though friendly, it is never overly demanding of your time, and will get along fine by itself during the day.

The Norwegian Forest Cat can adapt to nearly any household environment, and will not require constant attention from its owner. Though it is capable of amusing itself during the day, the owner of this breed should appeal to its hunting instincts by providing it with a few mouse-like toys. Also provide the Norwegian Forest Cat with a multi-tiered kitty condo, to satisfy its desire to climb and survey its territory from above. Though not as labor intensive as a Persian, this breed's owners will need to brush and comb it about once a week. During the late spring, this breed will lose its undercoat and outer guard hairs, which could cause some discomfort to those sensitive to cat hair.

Persian

Along with its kissing cousin the Himalayan, the Persian is widely considered to be the most popular of the cat breeds. A large, heavy-boned cat, the Persian has a strong muscled body, short powerful legs, and large feet. The characteristic head is wide and flat-faced, with stout cheeks and small ears. Its short muzzle and round, expressive, wide-set eyes give the Persian a truly unique look among cats. The thick, long coat comes in a wide variety of colors and patterns.

One of the oldest of cat breeds, the Persian may have first been seen in fifteenth-century Turkey, and is probably descended from the Angora. By the seventeenth century the breed was discovered by Italians traveling in Persia, and then brought to Europe, which at the time had no indigenous longhaired cat. Needless to say it was an immediate success.

A docile, affectionate, somewhat reserved cat, the Persian tends toward the quiet side. Unobtrusive to a fault, this breed deals well with an absentee owner, easily amusing itself during the day. Though sweet and loving toward its owner, the Persian can be aloof toward strangers, and may not deal well with lots of commotion or a group of active children. Much less active than other breeds, the Persian rarely jumps or leaps, and is rarely destructive or cross. For those looking for a serene cat who does not need constant attention, look no further.

The Persian needs a calm, non-confrontational environment and a laid-back, respectful owner looking for a placid pet. As this breed tends not to be very active or athletic, even the smallest apartment will suit it just fine. The owner of a Persian will need to comb his or her cat out every day to prevent matting of the long, thick coat. Those with small children might do better considering a more interactive breed. A scratching post, several toys, and lots of love is all the Persian should need to stay happy.

Mixed Breeds

Most of you probably adopted your kitten or cat from a shelter. If your cat is a mix of two pedigreed cats, it may be possible for you to identify what breeds her parents may have been. Some indicators are obvious; the wide, short face of the Persian or the distinct pointed coloration of the Siamese are both easy to spot, as are the curled ears of the American Curl or the stumpy tail of the Manx. Though you may not be able to properly identify what breeds went into the making of your cat, guessing at it can be a fun way of learning more about the breeds. And if you have strong indicators of the breed mix, you'll be able to research those breeds and the behavioral profiles, helping you to better predict your own cat's behaviors and reactions.

Most cat owners probably own a generic cat, better known as a "domestic." Veterinarians usually refer to three basic types: the *domestic shorthair*, the *domestic medium-length hair*, and the *domestic longhair*. All tend to be of similar size and weight, though substantial variations can occur (especially if the cat is overfed!).

Colors
Color patterns in cats apply to both purebred and domestics. These include:

Solid
Any solid color such as black, white, gray or brown.

Tabby
Any cat with a striped, spotted or mackerel pattern. Tabbies can also have blocks of white, or white "boots" or chests.

Bi-color
Two solid colors, usually gray-and-white or orange-and-white.

Tricolor
Cats with three distinct color patterns. These include the calico, with blocks of orange, black and white, and sometimes with added white accents or tabby markings, and the tortoiseshell, which has colors woven together instead of in distinct blockish patterns. The tortoiseshell can also have white accents.

Tuxedo
A black cat with a white chest, who can also have white boots. This is the classic "Sylvester" cat endlessly searching for his Tweety bird.

Pointed
A solid-colored cat with darker shades of the same color at her "points," or her ears, tail, muzzle and paws. The Siamese is a classic pointed cat.

Your Cat's Unique Personality

Breed and coat length alone do not a cat make. Two cats from the same litter with near identical appearances can display completely different personalities from a very early age, supporting the idea that the genesis of personality is more complex than simply a combination of breed, species and environment. Some cats are brave and sociable, while others choose to bestow their attentions on only a few trusted souls. One may love endless play while another tires of it quickly, preferring to just sit on her owner's desk and purr. Some can't get enough attention, while others quickly reach their fill, opting for just the occasional head pat.

For each cat then, there is a unique personality that as a natural owner you must become attuned to in order to truly understand what makes her tick. To begin to understand her personality, you should first learn about your cat's species-specific predispositions, and her unique breed profile. Once you understand how these help define her basic behavior and unique needs, you can add that indefinable ingredient— her own distinctive idiosyncrasies —to arrive at a clear feel for her.

Your Cat's History

A huge part of your cat's personality will be defined by her personal history—what distinctive experiences she has had from birth that have helped mold who she is. Let's look at the key elements that make up her history:

Origins

Where you acquired your cat can have a great effect on her personality. For instance, did she come from a caring breeder who raises kittens in her home, with plenty of socialization with people and other pets, a kitten not put up for sale until at least seven or eight weeks of age? If so, your cat will most likely show good confidence, and not shy away from strangers. Or, did you get her at a local shelter? If this is the case, your cat may have experienced some level of trauma at some point in her life, trauma that can play a role in her future temperament. For instance, an adult cat adopted from a shelter has almost certainly been either surrendered up by a previous owner, or else found and turned in. In either case the cat has suffered separation anxiety and a massive change in lifestyle, two things they hate.

If you acquired a cat from an advertisement in the classifieds, her breeding and upbringing might be suspect. Often private sellers or adopters unload kittens that their female cats have unintentionally birthed; these kittens often leave their mothers far too early, sometimes as soon as five weeks of age. When this happens, the kittens do not receive enough time to socialize with other cats and learn proper sibling etiquette; this can result in a painfully shy, antisocial animal. If at all possible, avoid "backyard breeders" and people unloading a litter that should not have been birthed in the first place. If you did acquire a cat at a young age, know that she may have trouble interacting with people or other pets, and adjust the environment accordingly. That means not adopting other cats or dogs unless your resident cat has proved to be accepting to other pets. Ignoring this will cause undue stress for your cat, resulting in misbehaviors.

A cat rescued off the street by you may have suffered even more than a shelter cat. She has not only been separated from her owner, but also accosted by all manner of threats, from inclement weather and a shortage of food to cars, dogs, other cats, or even uncaring persons with bad intentions. If your cat is one of these brave souls, odds are she may be a bit guarded around strangers or even you, at least for the first few months. Rescue cats require patient owners who allow the cats to come around in their own time.

If you have adopted a cat that has been used to an indoor/outdoor lifestyle, odds are she will continue to desire access to the outdoors. When denied this access the adult cat will almost certainly pine away for the old days in some fashion, perhaps meowing incessantly, pacing, scratching at the door, or trying to sneak out whenever the door opens. Destructive behavior can occur as well, a form of "redirected" stress that results not only in damaged carpets, furniture, drapes, etc., but also in erratic housetraining. Cats allowed outdoors often choose to eliminate there instead of in the litter box; as old habits die very hard in cats, the removal of this option can drive some cats bonkers. I'll discuss solutions to this issue later in the book; in the meantime be aware that most cats used to the outdoors will, when suddenly denied the privilege, most likely exhibit stress-related behaviors as a result.

Objective Evaluation of Your Cat

Once you develop a good understanding for your cat's physiology, origins, background, breed-specific characteristics and distinctive personality, it's time to objectively evaluate her overall demeanor and potential, and how well she interacts with her environment. This is important for one key reason: it will allow you to determine how assertive you can be with regard to your own interactions with your cat, with socializing with other persons and pets, with behavior modifications or training, and with environmental changes. Understanding what your cat can and cannot handle emotionally will help minimize stress levels, and thereby undesirable behavior and health problems. Remember: some cats are resilient and adaptable, while others abhor change and a busy, unpredictable social climate.

How the Home Influences the Cat/Owner Relationship

Your home is your cat's world. The unique parameters of this world will influence to a degree how she relates to you and others. For instance, if you live in a large home in a rural setting and allow your cat outdoor access, she will tend to be an explorer and become enamored with the limitless amount of stimuli available to her. This type of cat gets used to a high level of autonomy, and will not react well if required to surrender it. It's why adult indoor/outdoor cats adopted out to new owners have such a hard time adapting to indoor-only living, especially in a small apartment. I've seen many cats like this abandon their good house-training habits and become destructive and antisocial, purely as a reaction to this sudden loss of autonomy.

A cat allowed to roam outdoors will almost certainly come into conflict with other cats, and perhaps dogs and other animals. This makes future pet additions to the family problematic. Outdoor cats tend to also develop "street savvy"; caution and survival become the overriding concern, causing them to become more discerning and reserved around strangers, however friendly. Though not guaranteed, it's a good bet that cats allowed outside will be less sociable. When friends come over and your cat disappears, don't overreact, scoop the cat up, and force her to socialize. Let her find her own comfort zone. She may come out eventually; just understand why she is reticent.

Small homes or apartments mean a small territory for your cat. As cats tend to be quite territorial, filling a small space with many pets or people can be stressful for your little tiger. There is just so much allotted space; if you live in a small abode, realize that your cat will not have any areas to retreat to if and when hectic activity occurs. If forced to tolerate too much activity, your cat could act out in some way, so be aware of this. Avoid punishing your cat for unexpected, unusual behaviors (such as poor litter box use or fear aggression), when in all likelihood you have set up the environment to cause it.

The home should be a comfortable place for your cat. It should be safe, quiet, and predictable. And, there should be fun, stimulating things to do. Without enriching stimuli such as kitty condos, cardboard boxes filled with newspaper, toys or scratching posts, your cat will get bored, and may act out. This of course can adversely affect your relationship; to avoid this, be sure to read Secret Five: Enrich Your Cat's Environment.

Choosing a Cat

For those who do not yet have a cat or who are considering getting another, you'll need to decide upon which cat will be the best one for your lifestyle. I'll try to help you narrow down the search here.

Pedigreed?

Pedigreed cats have lineages that include only other purebred cats from
breeds accepted by a national or international cat association. They
have very predictable physical and behavioral profiles; a Persian has an
unmistakable look and temperament, as does a Sphynx or Ocicat. The
look or behavior of a particular cat may appeal to you; if so, and you
can afford the price, by all means seek out a responsible breeder and go
for it. Purchasing from a respected breeder ensures you a great chance
of getting a healthy, well-adjusted, beautiful cat that comes with a
health guarantee and at least some of the required vaccinations. Caring
breeders are devoted to their breeds, and make sure their cats go to
qualified homes. The downsides to buying a pedigreed cat include cost
(high), and availability (low). Also, with the smaller gene pool and possible inbreeding that occurs with some rare breeds, you can run the risk
of hereditary abnormalities affecting health or behavior. If a breeder has
a good reputation, these risks are minimized, however.

There is, of course, the chance of finding a pedigreed cat at a shelter.
Usually pedigreed cats given up for various reasons will be affordable,
and just as beautiful. But more often than not they will be adult cats;
you'll miss out on the fun of kittenhood, and could be inheriting
behavior or health problems from someone else. Quality shelters usually
weed out cats with health or behavior issues, though, so don't ignore
this option.

If you desire a pedigreed cat, which breed should you choose? To
decide, you should study the over forty breeds of cat available by reading
books, magazines and website breed profiles. Once you narrow down
your potential selections to just a few breeds, you'll then need to locate a
few reputable breeders and spend a bit of time with some cats, to get a
feel for their unique behavioral and physical profiles. Apart from esthetic
appeal, you'll want to consider how a particular breed might fit in to
your home; if you have several children and an active, unpredictable
home, consider an active, outgoing breed like a Siamese, Sphynx or
Tonkinese. If you live alone in a predictable, calm environment, more

reserved breeds such as the Persian or Ragdoll might be the ticket. Also remember that shorthaired breeds tend to be a bit more outgoing than their longhaired counterparts. But also realize that, if you get a pedigreed kitten, she will in all likelihood adapt fairly well to nearly any environment you provide to her, so long as it is safe, and considerate of her needs as a cat.

Mixed Breed or "Domestic" Cats

There are thousands of unwanted kittens and cats available for adoption at any given time. Many of them will be euthanized for lack of a home to go to. The reason? Simple: some owners let their unneutered cats outside, allowing them to breed and produce litters of kittens in need of homes. Unfortunately there aren't enough homes on the planet available for the numbers of kittens being produced. Unlike puppies, which usually get placed quite quickly, kittens and adult cats do not find homes so readily, due to their sheer numbers, and to the difficulty of placing adult cats into new environments. Adult shelter cats often are there because they have been surrendered up for bad behaviors, or because people simply don't want them anymore; these cats often are euthanized before an appropriate home can be found for them.

If you are looking for a new cat, consider rescuing a kitten or young adult cat from a reputable shelter. They are a bargain compared to pedigreed cats; you'll probably have to pay for neutering and vaccinations, plus a small additional adoption fee. Shelters almost always filter out the sick, aggressive or behaviorally challenged cats, ensuring that most adoptees will be happy and healthy.

Acquiring a cat or kitten from the classifieds can be a riskier venture. You won't know if the pet is healthy, or if she has had any kind of temperament testing. The motives of the seller are also in question; intentional breeding for profit by "backyard breeders" should always be discouraged. Acquiring a cat this way also encourages the sellers to continue breeding cats, something that needs to be discouraged, not encouraged.

There are a few disadvantages to adopting a domestic cat. First, you may not find out much about her history, and what her past home environment was like. If the pet's parents had psychological or physiological problems, these can be passed on, and you won't have any way of knowing. Buying from a reputable breeder reduces these problems considerably. But most good shelters do a great job of putting only healthy, well-adjusted cats up for adoption, minimizing these important concerns.

Cat or Kitten?

If given a choice, I'd choose a kitten over an adult cat. They are cute as buttons, and basically untouched by adverse experiences, making it easy for a kitten to acclimate to your home environment. You won't have many glaring behavior problems to modify, and will have the chance to raise her in the best way possible. She'll be treated well right from the start and given the best foods and health care, preventing any problems down the line.

When you adopt an adult cat, you inherit health or behavioral problems she may have developed along the way. But they do have some advantages over kittens. First, being fully grown (or nearly so), there are no surprises regarding size, coat length, or temperament. All of these are already well established; what you see is what you get. Plus, you get the chance to save a cat from the grim reaper's grip. Remember: many more adult cats are euthanized than kittens. And an adult cat usually has fairly stable litter box habits (though always expect a short readjustment period once home), making the transition a bit easier. An adult will need a bit less attention than will a more needy kitten, making ownership for a busy person easier.

If you decide on a kitten, consider getting two. They will bond and keep each other company while you are away, preventing boredom that can lead to stress-related misbehaviors. If getting an adult cat, only get two if they are siblings, or if they have lived with each other for years. If you adopt two adult cats unfamiliar to each other, you may create a

stressful, contentious environment for both of them, one involving
bickering over territory, attention, litter box and food issues; instead
of enjoying the experience, you could end up stressed and dissuaded,
leading to the surrender of one cat. Remember, adult cats are not always
very accepting of other pets.

Avoiding Impulse

Don't make an impulsive decision to acquire a cat. It should be a well-
thought out, unemotional choice, and not one made on the spur of the
moment. Those who get a cat in this way often discover early on that
they aren't really prepared for pet ownership; this often leads to surrender of the pet to a shelter, making a subsequent adoption more difficult. Think it out well in advance; talk it over with your family, and do
your homework. Find a reputable shelter in the area, and visit it several
times just to acquaint yourself with the cats. Then make the decision
based on which cat will best fit into your lifestyle. Don't let little children
make the choice, and don't fall for a hard luck case (unless she is a great
little pet with the right personality). Being selfish and exacting in the
beginning will allow you to be giving and unselfish later on.

SECRET TWO:
Embrace a Feline Attitude and Awareness

To experience what it's really like to be in harmony with your cat, develop what I call *"effective feline empathy."* In a more common parlance, you should *"be the cat."* Instead of trying to turn your cat into a proxy human (as so many owners do), you can turn yourself into a proxy cat, and in the process connect with her on a deeper level. If you can learn as much as possible about how your cat relates to her world, and understand the real motivations for why she does what she does, you'll take a giant leap forward in becoming a "natural" cat owner.

Living in the Feline Moment

Your cat has an awareness of her world that dwarfs our own. When you come home and greet her, you see her threading in and out of your legs, looking at you, perhaps meowing a *"hello, about time you got back."* But she is also smelling all you have done, the people you have seen, the food you have eaten, the cats and dogs who might have crossed your path—basically anything that you have come across that day. While you pet her she listens to the chickadee rustling in the rhododendron outside your bedroom window, and the squirrel trying to find the chestnut he'd misplaced. She is aware at a higher level, with a real-time empathy for her environment we can only imagine. She watches you closely and is in the moment, reading your body language, listening to your tone, wondering why you are doing whatever it is you happen to be doing, and when you'll be feeding her. Though she does have a vague sense of past and future, she prefers the present, because that is what matters most.

To *"be the cat,"* one of the first things to do is to enter that feline moment as best and as often as you can. Instead of getting lost in thought or becoming too involved in talking to or petting your cat, consider trying it her way. Become observant, attentive, curious. Watch her body posture, her explorations, her priorities. Touch her when she appears accessible and open. Watch as she explores the home, and try to reason out just what it is she finds so fascinating, odd, or even disturbing at that moment. Guess at what she wants or wonders.

For instance, when the neighbor's dog barks, do her ears perk up? When the timer on your microwave goes off, does she react? How about when you use the electric can opener on a can of cat food? Does she come running to the sound?

Part of living in the feline moment involves understanding body posture. For instance, do you know what the classic signs of a scared or distressed cat are? Her ears will flatten, her back will most likely arch, and her tail will thrash unpredictably. Pupils widen, and her hair may puff or stand on end. She may hiss, yowl or bare her fangs, and either retreat or go on the offensive if feeling trapped. If you see any or all of these signs, know that trouble is afoot.

Most of you can tell when your cat is content. She may knead you with her paws, purr, meow or chirp, or sprawl and stretch lazily onto her side. And she may press her face into you or rub against you repeatedly (also a marking behavior—she does own you after all). Her tail will probably point straight up.

Play aggression? Common with developing youngsters still learning the social ropes, your cat might playfully pounce on you, bat at you, or even half-heartedly bite or scratch. Sometimes her paws will wrap around your hand or leg. Though fairly harmless, play aggression can sometimes turn into real aggression if the owner encourages it or crosses the "comfort" line with the cat. The best solution is to avoid rough play entirely, and in its place substitute toys and teaser wands, directing her stalking skills toward these. Any other enriching activities or objects (such as paper-filled boxes or multi-tiered platforms) will keep her busy and redirect that playful energy.

The point is, by being empathetic to the motivations for your cat's behavior, you'll know how to react to it properly, and how to channel it into positive outcomes. Above all, never punish your cat for play aggression. Remember: she is not a dog, and does not react to correction the same way. Cats will become fearful of any retribution, and will hold grudges for a long time! Better to avoid over-the-top behavior through prevention or redirection.

How about *your* body posture? Just as you can and should read hers, she readily reads yours. You can give her the right signals or the wrong signals with your body, voice and actions. For instance, rushing at your cat will almost certainly scare her and perhaps cause a defensive reaction. Running *away* from her may incite play aggression or some other undesirable stalking behavior. Yelling or hitting are absolute no-no's, as are stomping your feet or any overly aggressive activity. Towering over her may also intimidate, as might random, erratic behavior. As far as body posture goes, present yourself in the most inviting, calm manner possible, with predictable movements and a gentle, supportive voice.

Territory

Space means a lot to cats. Wild felines covet it; without the right size territory they cannot catch enough prey, meet the right mates, raise young or ensure détente with competing cats. By properly spacing themselves out, they guarantee that all will have an ample buffer zone, a reliable source of food and mates, and a lifestyle as free as possible from interspecies stress.

Territory therefore becomes not something to greedily hoard, but a necessary survival tool which most solitary felines instinctively hold in high regard. Try to pack too many cats (or cats with too many people and/or dogs) into too small a space and you may be asking for behavioral troubles.

Compared to dogs, who tolerate sharing space with those they consider pack members, the domestic cat is much more discriminating about territorial issues. Your cat will share your home with you and others it knows and accepts as "kin," but will most likely be suspicious of strangers or strange animals coming into their own "hoods." When confronted by strangers, the shy cat disappears under a bed, while even the outgoing cat will check out the visitors prudently, perhaps deciding to stay at a distance for a bit. If well socialized, most happy cats will interact, albeit not with the same trust that they would with you. It's normal and natural; unless your cat attacks strangers, just let her decide on her level of interaction. That's the natural feline way to be.

Cats define their territories by marking them with scratches, secretions from scent glands on the body, urine, and even feces (though not commonly). In the wild, cats bury feces in order to mask their presence from predators, or to avoid inciting conflict with another cat whose territory might overlap. That's why domestics are so darned easy to litter box train!

When your cat rubs up against you repeatedly, she is not just saying "*I love you*," but is claiming "ownership" and acceptance by rubbing her scent onto you. She also lays out her home territory very precisely with scent rubbings (and the occasional furniture scratch). She develops well-traveled pathways throughout the home, then "patrols" them regularly throughout the day, establishing resting spots and lookout positions (usually windows and high perches). Whether you know it or not, she has your home mapped out, gridded, protected and claimed.

To become that natural cat owner, watch your cat when she patrols her territory. Notice where she perches and rests, and how predictably she frequents them. If you have two or more cats, notice how each cat has her own favorite spots, and how they often take turns sharing territory in an almost "time-share" kind of way; instead of each using only small parts of the home, they simply "schedule" in their own timed territorial periods. This avoids fights and allows harmony among pets that ordinarily would not crave many of their own kind in the same space.

Remember that to a cat, territory is four-dimensional, including time of day. That means she can inhabit parts of the home you cannot, such as the top of the fridge or armoire, beneath the sofa, on the banister, atop the entertainment center—nearly anywhere her agile body will take her. This helps manage territorial concerns, especially in multiple-cat families. One cat might dominate the upper reaches while the other trolls around at ground level. They can then alternate, meeting up when they like or staying out of each other's way.

Be sure to respect your cat's need for a well-defined territory. Avoid bringing unpredictable crowds into the home, especially persons who insist upon seeking out and petting your cat, who might not wish to immediately socialize with them. Also resist letting strange animals in, like your neighbor's six month-old Great Dane puppy, or your cousin's ferret. If people are coming over, let them know to allow the cat to set her own agenda regarding contact; if she decides to bail under the bed, so be it. And do *not* let children pester her! Though usually curious and well-meaning, the spontaneity of kids can drive adult cats bonkers, and can even lead to scratching or biting.

Let Your Cat's Personality Set the Tone of Your Relationship

I had a client once who, after owning dogs for twenty years, decided to try a cat instead. His old terrier mix had passed away, and he just didn't feel up to the work involved with a new puppy or young adult dog. But he still wanted pet company, so off to the shelter he went. Instead of getting a brace of kittens (as I had advised him to do), he fell victim to a pretty adult domestic longhair, surrendered because of a home filled with kids and hectic activity. Evidently she had scratched and bitten an eight-year-old after being cornered under an end table; she just couldn't cope with the hectic environment, and needed adult calmness and a quiet home.

He fell for this pretty little hard luck case and took her home. Told by the shelter to be patient and loving with her, he dutifully obeyed, and became the model of patience and tolerance. But after a week of her hiding and avoiding, he decided to use a little "dog" logic on her to try to get her out of her shell. I'd suggested feeding her at prescribed times, to develop a routine that would build some level of cat/owner contact; the association of food to human attention can help desensitize shy cats and get them to relax in a person's presence. It worked, to a degree; she'd come out from a hiding place and eat while he sat quietly in a chair nearby, talking gently. But soon the dog logic took over: he tried to pet and hold her. Thinking that she would accept him faster if he could just get her past the initial fear of being handled, he grabbed her as she flitted by him one day, only to be bitten and scratched in the process.

With my help he found an elderly cat lover willing to take the trau-matized orphan. We then went back to the shelter and brought home two eleven-week-old domestic shorthair siblings filled with courage and attitude; the brother and sister fit right in to the man's home, and were fetching mouse toys back to my client within three days of being in the new environment.

Moral? First, don't treat your cat like a dog. More important, you must allow your cat to set the "rules of engagement" in the home, based upon her personality and what she can tolerate. Once a cat's personality is set (something that happens quite quickly, in my opinion, evidencing itself as early as six to eight weeks), it's not going to change all that much. You can certainly train your cat to tolerate and enjoy new expe-riences and stimuli, but you won't be able to substantially alter her demeanor. Cats simply do not adapt as well as humans or dogs, and shouldn't be expected to.

To that end, once you have identified your cat's unique personality, it is vital for you to let that personality determine just how you and the rest of your family will interact with her. For instance, if she is an out-going, gregarious little firebrand, you can have the confidence to know that she should be able to handle new people and perhaps even other pets, and tolerate moderate fluctuations in routine and environment. A brave happy cat will enjoy being tested by new stimuli, and may love learning tricks. She may even be open to learning to wear a harness, allowing you to take her for short walks in the yard or even around the block. (I'll discuss walking your cat later; for now, know that it is something to be started early in a cat's life, and not once the cat is years old).

If she is by nature timid and shy, your cat will need more stability in her life. I recommend a gentler, easier style of cat ownership with the demure feline, one that includes a well-established routine and more predictable social surroundings. Try not to overload her with unsolicited attention from guests, and never compel her to enter into social situations. Let *her* decide when to come out and greet. When she does, praise her and consider rewarding with a treat. But remember to let her initiate contact!

This should apply even to you. When home, wait for those moments when your demure cat comes over for a head rub or pet, then reinforce her pluck with gentle attention. Be sure not to overdo it, and let her walk away when she has had enough. If you do, she'll be more likely to ask for more attention soon. With timid cats, it's a patient process of desensitization and gentle reinforcement that gets results.

Rescues or adopted strays are by necessity cautious creatures. They have to be, considering what they may have been through. Disease, catfights, dog, raccoon or coyote predation, cars, scavenging for food—survival tends to breed suspicion and vigilance, and your rescue or stray will reflect that. Relations with you may be tentative for a while; accept that, and don't push yourself upon the cat. Create a safe, predictable home environment, with little commotion and all the comforts, including at least one litter box, and fresh food and water. Realize that street habits may take a while to dissipate; she may pine away for the freedom of the streets, which, though dangerous, was all she knew. And she will most likely be reserved around strangers, and have a short fuse regarding being handled. When she decides enough is enough, respect that. Push the handling and you risk evoking an aggressive response.

With any cat, be patient, predictable, and perceptive: the "three Ps" if you will. Taking this attitude will put the ball in her court and allow you to calmly determine what level of interaction is best. Her personality is the key that establishes the ground rules; ascertain this and the rest is easy.

Cats Never Forget

One last point. Unlike dogs, who have the ability to forgive and forget owner blunders, cats tend to remember mistakes for a long time. I had a cat in college who was accidentally kicked by a friend walking down a flight of steps; though a friendly cat, she never got over the incident, and would flee at the very sight of my poor guilty friend, despite many proffered treats. Those who physically abuse their cats in any way will close the door forever on intimacy. Even verbal scolding can frighten some cats enough to permanently brand the scolder as a persona non grata.

Your cat will hold a grudge against you if you abuse it in any way. The same will hold for other people or pets who create a potentially fearful situation for your cat. The key is the cat's interpretation, and not the actual event. A big slobbery dog that ambles into your home and tries to befriend your kitten may mean well, but will nonetheless be seen by your cat as a carnivorous monster hell-bent on destruction. So, choose your emotions carefully when around your cat; avoid losing your temper, and never hit her. And whatever you do, don't step on her tail!

Calm Indifference

Watch your cat interact with someone she trusts. Even though she is clearly comfortable with the person, she still takes a somewhat haughty attitude about the event, as if she is saying *"yes, yes… I love you too, but I'm not really in the mood to do a back-flip over it right now if you don't mind."* She rarely lets her emotions get the best of her, and instead takes it all in stride. Cool, calm, classy and collected; a very cattish way to be.

To "be the cat," you should reflect this laid-back attitude. I call it "calm indifference," a slightly aloof bearing which, though clearly respectful and polite, remains somewhat independent of the moment, almost as if you had other more pressing issues on your mind. This pensive demeanor will actually attract your cat more than will a more frenetic, bubbly, hyper-focused one. It's how most cats behave, and you should copy it.

Create a Parental Partnership

Unlike the sociable, pack-oriented dog, the more sovereign nature of the cat requires owners to adopt a different method of "group management." Instead of using the pack hierarchy as a tool for maintaining social stability and order in the home, the natural cat owner cleverly fosters a "perpetual state of parenthood" with his or her cat, to maintain a semblance of authority without seeming to do so. Becoming a revered parent in your cat's eyes is a vital ingredient in preventing undesirable behaviors, and in encouraging a close familial relationship with an animal known for its independent, self-governing nature. Want to get along fabulously? Then "be the cat" mama!

The Social Life of Cats

As most of you know, most wild and domestic cats are by nature aloof, independent hunters who rely upon stealth and an egoistic sense of independence to survive. Unlike canines who rely upon teamwork to take down large prey, most felines go it alone, stalking and killing prey that is on average smaller than themselves.

But felines are not purely isolationist by nature. For example, female lions and their young form "prides," lorded over by a dominant male. They hunt and socialize together, raise cubs communally, and collectively guard their territories against other marauding lions. Cheetah brothers often ally with each other for hunting purposes. And feral domestic cats often come together in large colonies whenever a consistent, plentiful food source is present. Lured by the abundance of food, these survivors form a loose social structure that tolerates a fairly dense population of cats. Communal rearing of kittens occurs, as does familial collectives of related females, who are known to socialize with each other quite readily. Unneutered males usually do not participate in the socializing due to territorial stresses, though neutered males can and do participate. And even rudimentary hierarchical behavior can be observed among feral colony members, evidenced by ritualistic "rubbing." The more a cat is rubbed, the higher up she is in the hierarchy.

In all, social behavior in feral cat colonies tends to closely reflect familial arrangements seen among siblings and their mothers. This familial bias seems to support the evolutionary notion that family members "selfishly" support the passing on of their own genes over those of strangers.

Clearly, your cat is capable of social interaction with both humans and other cats, especially when the supply of food in your home is stable and plentiful. As long as ample space exists to placate your cat's needs, you should see a reasonable amount of social cooperation between not only you and your cat, but between the cats in your home.

A key to cat socialization is the perception of familial ties. If you have two sibling cats, for example, raised together from kittenhood, odds are strong that they will get along fabulously. Why? Besides recognizing their hereditary tie, they have been together since birth, and have imprinted upon each other. Almost the same social bond forms with two kittens from different litters raised together from early on; they bond quickly and consider each other family. They learn social skills together, and feel comfortable in each other's presence.

Bring new cats or persons into the home of your resident cat, though, and you complicate the issue somewhat. There is no perceived familial bond; the "interloper" cat appears as an invader and will often be shunned or even attacked by your established cat. The same can go for new people; I know of many cases in which, upon moving in with their cat-loving partner, the unsuspecting new person gets the cold shoulder or even a hiss, bite or scratch as a welcome.

What can I say; it's just the way some cats are. These reserved cats do often come around in time; it just takes patience and a willingness on the behalf of the new person not to be too proactive in trying to win the cat over. My advice to new people coming into a cat home is to let the cat decide when the time is right to run up the white flag. The process can, of course, be helped along; the new person can feed the cat each day, passively offer treats and toys, and respond to the cat's approach with quiet talk and a light rub of the head. In general it is the "butterfly lighting upon your shoulder" concept; surrender, and let the cat come to you.

A cat who does not possess the desire to socialize at all may have been taken from her litter at too early an age. Often six-week-old kittens are adopted out to willing families who know little about the need for kittens to play with other kittens at this young age, so they miss the opportunity to learn valuable social skills that will stay with them for life. They need to interact with their mothers and siblings at this stage; denied this, they often become reclusive, even for a cat. In the best of all worlds, a kitten should not leave her mother and littermates until the tenth to twelfth week. Allowed to intermingle with her family during this crucial impressionable age, the kitten will be far more likely to tolerate and even welcome cats or other people into her life later on.

Who Are You to Your Cat?

Unlike the dominance hierarchy of the dog, where ideally an owner establishes him- or herself as a patrician leader of the group, cats recognize no such established pecking order. They are autonomous masters of their own providence, obeying a narcissistic need to call their own shots. It's part of the reason we love and respect them so much.

If your cat considers herself to be her own boss, then where do you fit in? Are you simply a feeder, or an innkeeper? Just someone nice enough to provide meals and entertainment? Who *are* you, really?

To answer that question, let's examine cats in the wild again. With most cat species, the mother has an innate parental authority over her kittens, which grants her the power to touch, clean, discipline, teach, love, guide and feed them at her discretion. This natural-born maternal status serves to keep the newborns safe and healthy, and in the process allows learning to occur. The kittens learn to hunt, socialize, bury waste, keep clean, recognize territorial boundaries—a myriad of feline survival skills. The mother's innate authority and status allow this to happen.

Once her young are capable of surviving on their own, the feline mother rebukes her offspring and sends them packing. She rejects them outright, despite their desire to stay for the free lunches and maternal attention. Cruel? Maybe. But by forcing the issue, she ensures that they will go out and create litters of their own so the species can continue. Kicking the adolescent litter out also allows her to birth and raise her next litter of kittens, an impossibility if the previous litter lingers.

What if she never kicked them out? What would the social dynamic be? Odds are her offspring, though quickly reaching physical maturity, would remain somewhat "childlike" in mindset. They would maintain much of their sociable, kitten-like behavior, and would continue to see their mother as an authority figure and provider. In effect they would remain perpetual kittens, with an allegiance to their mother's elder standing and celebrity. She would maintain maternal jurisdiction over them, and they would remain beholden to her for many of their needs, including food and affection.

This is the ideal model for cat owners to emulate. Most cat experts agree that owners who become "surrogate cat mothers" to their cats have the best chance at harmony in the home. This is especially true when the cat is acquired as an eight- to ten-week-old kitten, during an impressionable, socially vigorous period. Somewhat confused and distraught by the sudden absence of her mother and littermates, the kitten naturally seeks out solace and affection from whoever is available. That of course would be the new owner, along with any other people or pets in the home. As I have stated before (and will many times again no doubt), this is also a stellar reason for adopting two kittens at the same time; they'll help comfort each other through the trauma of leaving their litter and mother, and will encourage each other to take social chances that alone they might not ordinarily have the courage to take. When one sees the other doing something daring, she is drawn into the activity out of sheer competitive zeal.

The Eternal Kitty/Child

When a kitten goes from her mother and littermates to your home, she immediately feels a bit lonely and befuddled, and will naturally look to you for solace. You will provide her with it, of course, along with everything a mother would: affection, grooming, food, guidance, and knowledge about the environment. The kitten quickly transfers her maternal needs from her birth mother to you. You will hopefully *not* be kicking her out of the home at four months of age, as might a cat mother living in a feral colony. You will provide her with a home and maternal love and care, forever. By constantly being available as the "mommy," you forestall the normal social maturation process that would occur in nature, and instead create a perpetual state of "need." Kittens sleep with mom, greet her happily, and look to her expectantly for food and contact; by staying with you, the surrogate mom, these behaviors never really subside. They do lessen somewhat over time, but never quite dissipate. Though your cat will mature, she will always think of you as Mom.

This is not a bad thing, but rather a valuable tool in managing her behavior. While she might consider misbehaving toward another cat or person, she won't with you, because you are the über-parent, the provider of all things good. And if you acquire your cat as a kitten, she will think of you as a mother without any prodding on your part. All you need do is recognize it when you see it; her desire to be with you is based in large part on her perception of you as a providing parent figure.

Sibling Owners

Not all cat/owner relationships can follow the mother/offspring model. Say for instance you adopt a two-year-old stray used to living the hard life out on the street. She has been on her own, roaming the neighborhood, hunting birds and mice, eating cat and dog food left out overnight, rummaging through garbage cans, dodging cars and raccoons, and who knows what else. She's fought off other cats, produced three litters, been infested with parasites—the whole hard luck story. You take this trouper in and give her a home, spend five hundred in veterinary care, clean her up, feed her, give her love. What kind of relationship will you have with her?

Rather than being seen as a mother, you will at first probably be considered a "person of interest," someone who provides food and shelter and a safe, quiet lifestyle free from the dangers of the street. Not necessarily to be trusted yet, but definitely an improvement.

Gradually, as the routine of the home is established, the cat will learn to trust and rely on your consistent charity and companionship. If you play it cool and don't expect too much at first, she will eventually come around. Maybe a rub or a meow at dinnertime, a sharing of the bed, or a careful sniff of your leg while you are sitting watching television. However when she does decide to break bread with you, she will. This is the beginning of a relationship that more closely resembles sibling-to-sibling than mother and child. The cat will see you as an equal, sharing a comfortable, well-stocked territory. Ultimately you will be considered a worthy brother or sister, someone to trust and share the great new digs with.

As a "sibling" owner, you won't have quite the same relationship as you might when raising a kitten or young cat. Any kind of behavior modification you attempt will not have the authoritative weight of "mommy dearest" behind it; you'll have to be a bit more democratic about how you interact. For instance, with a cat who sees you as a maternal figure, you can pick her up almost any time you wish, and even groom her or examine her for parasites. With a rescued adult cat who sees you as a sibling, you may or may not have the authority to pick her up whenever you want; you simply do not have the jurisdiction to do so. You have to be a bit more patient and clever about it; instead of seeking her out and lifting her up, try to lure her over onto your lap with a toy or treat. Or just wait for her to invite herself over. Odds are she probably has developed a pattern for when she likes physical interaction; just wait for it, then casually examine her.

Though not necessarily as easy or rewarding as the maternal model of cat ownership, the sibling model works quite well, and is certainly preferable to a combative, confrontational relationship. And though most adult strays and rescues will think of you as a sibling rather than a mom, you will have an additional power that brothers and sisters don't have: the power of the food dish!

Guidelines for Creating the Parental Partnership

Luckily, you won't have to jump through hoops to convince your cat that you are her parent. If you acquired her as a kitten or young cat, she probably already thinks of you as such. It's enough for you to simply understand that she is thinking of you as a mother figure, and that her actions will often reflect this. She will be more playful and affectionate with you than others, and should readily come to you when called. She will be quite tolerant of petting and handling, and will search for you if you happen to go missing for a while. And she will greet you happily when you come home, and choose to snuggle up with you on the bed or sofa. She may groom you, or even knead at you with her paws, an instinctive action used by kittens on their mothers to stimulate lactation. This is a classic indicator that your cat thinks of you as Mom.

Whatever a kitten would do with her mother, she will probably do with you. You'll have a good amount of influence on her behavior, and will certainly be the "go-to" person for her in the home. All things in moderation, however. Let her set the tone of the relationship, and remember that she is not a dog!

Feeding will serve as reinforcement of your maternal influence, provided you feed on a schedule (more on that in Secret Six: Keep Your Cat Healthy and Safe). Grooming her will also help, as a cat's mother spends time cleaning her kittens.

With a cat acquired as an adult, you'll probably notice that she will be less needy and not nearly as preoccupied with your actions. She'll interact with you on her terms, and then wander off. Playtime will be fun, but when it's over, it's over. This is the sibling model; though brothers and sisters socialize and play, they can also grow weary of the rivalry. If your adult cat models this sibling relationship, when she does seek out her own space, respect her parity with you and let her be. If you sense this more mature, less childish demeanor in your cat, treat her like a sibling, and enjoy this special brand of camaraderie reserved for brothers and sisters.

SECRET FOUR:

Educate Your Cat

Educate a cat? Surely you jest! Truth be told, much of the "education" that occurs during a cat/owner relationship happens to us and not the kitty, especially for newbie owners. Learning how to best set up your home for the cat, what routine fits her best, what to feed, and many other factors take a bit of time for an owner to key in on.

Unlike dogs, who come into the home needing an education in housetraining, basic behavior and manners, cats come into our lives nearly self-sufficient. They usually have basic litter box habits right away, and quickly learn the demeanor of the home and those living in it. Many cat owners mistakenly assume then that their felines need no additional training, or that the very idea of teaching a cat new behaviors is an affront to their independent natures.

Natural cat owners don't make that mistake. They know that for a cat to be happy, she must learn to best cope with the home environment she's been placed into.

Knowledge Breeds Confidence

An important ingredient to any pet/owner relationship lies in creating a sense of confidence in the pet, to ensure trust and understanding between you. When your cat trusts you, so much more is possible; you can handle her without conflict, and know that she'll probably be more open to contact with others. Confidence breeds ease and a relaxed air about the home, which in turn creates the curiosity and poise all caring owners want to see in their cats. And for your cat to gain confidence, you have to do more than be kind and allow her to set the tone of the relationship; you have to stimulate her mind.

The better a cat understands her world, the more appealing her life becomes. Understanding your expectations and feeling at ease with her environment reduces the chances that stress or anxiety will seep into her life and cause behavioral issues. Remember, prevention is the best way to avoid cat problems; by helping to create a confident mindset in your cat, you will avert a host of undesirable issues down the line, from antisocial behavior or housetraining setbacks to destructive behavior, or even stress-related medical concerns.

Smarter Is Nicer

Any cat with a larger range of response due to a broader information base will be calmer and more amiable than one always confronted with strange unknowns, resulting in indecision and anxiety. The same goes for us too; when your boss asks you to take charge of a project and you have the confidence and knowledge to do so, you get the job done in a relaxed fashion. But when the task is foreign to you, stress seeps in and causes all manner of problems and potential conflict.

The cat who knows what to expect from the varying stimuli in her life will take most things in stride, without becoming nervous or reactive. This self-assured attitude translates to a happier, more socially motivated cat. The more she knows about her home, the nicer she'll be to you and the others in the home.

What Every Cat Should Know

Just what kind of knowledge are we talking about? The basics are always the first place to start. One of the very first things to teach your cat is where her litter box is. It sounds silly, but everyone needs to know where the commode is, yes? And when a new cat comes into a home, odds are the litter box will be a new one filled with clean litter, with no previous cat scent in it. Your cat won't scent it out automatically, so you'll need to show her where it is. Once she sees and touches the litter, she'll instinctively know what to do.

She'll need to know where her food and water dishes are, and where you have put her scratching posts (I recommend two per cat, of varied design). And don't forget to introduce her to the other members of the household; let her approach each person on her own; they can offer treats, or simply hang back and let her investigate at her own speed.

With regard to other pets in the home, it's a good idea to introduce them gradually. For the first few days, restrict the new cat to one room, while the other pets have the run of the rest of the home. They will smell and hear each other right away, but not be confronted with each other just yet. Then, if you can, open the door and place a baby gate or similar fenced barrier up, with a temporary, pinned-up curtain blocking the top opening. This will allow the new cat to see, smell, hear and nose up to the resident pets (who are hopefully well socialized and curious, and not nasty). There will probably be some hissing and defensive posturing; it's normal, so don't panic. Keep the arrangement at this stage for two or three days, or until it appears they are content with each other's presence. Then let the new cat have the run of the home, and let them work out their territorial arrangement. If the resident pet is a dog, make sure beforehand that he is cat tolerant, as it wouldn't be fair for you to subject a new cat to a feline-hating canine! Consider extending the barrier separation time a bit longer with a dog, to give them ample time to relax. The greatest risk, oddly enough, is often to the dog, who can get his eyes scratched by a fearful cat.

Then it's simply a matter of letting the new cat explore the home at her leisure, after you have rendered it safe for her to do so. That means hiding wires, securing doors and windows, removing any cleaners or potential toxins (including toxic plants, listed in Secret Six: Keep Your Cat Healthy and Safe), and preventing her from accessing areas of the home where she might get hurt, lost or disoriented. Don't let her get into the attic or any crawl spaces, and make sure you have no openings in the walls that she could slip into and disappear!

Teaching Her about Feeding Time

Cats are predators, and as such love a good meal. Part of basic education should be for you, the natural cat owner, to teach her where and when food will be available. My strong recommendation is to feed her at regularly scheduled times, to instill in her a predictable food drive. I'll speak more about food in Secret Six: Keep Your Cat Healthy and Safe. For now, it's vital for you to establish a comfortable, predictable feeding routine. You have already shown her where the food and water dishes are; next, teach her that at very specific times, wonderful, healthy food will be provided by you. Let her see you preparing the food and placing it into her dish. Then set it down in the proper place and praise her as she investigates it. Once she begins eating, give her some space and privacy to enjoy the meal and feel free from stress. I know I don't like to be stared at while I eat!

Scratching Post 101

You have already shown her where her scratching posts are; now make sure she uses them instead of your furniture. And she *will* need to scratch, not only to shed the outer sheaths on her claws and to keep them sharp, but as part of a desire to mark her territory. The actual scratches are supplemented by scent glands in her paws, which leave her telltale calling card wherever she rubs them. She'll like to scratch as part of a morning stretching regimen as well, one of many routine behaviors she loves to perform.

Choose scratching posts that are tall enough for your cat to get a full stretch on. Twenty-eight to thirty inches high should be fine, but no shorter. Regarding material, most cats like sisal hemp, though anything with a rough texture should work. Some cats like carpeting, while others prefer a ropier medium; if one doesn't work, try another.

Location is key, so don't make the mistake of locating the posts in hidden areas of the home. Remember your cat is marking, and as such wants to scratch publicly. Placing one in your living room and one in the bedroom (or wherever the cat sleeps) should work nicely. You can even splurge and purchase a "kitty condo," a multi-level carpeted structure with perches, box enclosures and resting surfaces that cats love to scratch, explore and relax on. Placing one of these in your living room will give your cat or cats a fun place to call their own.

Encourage her to use the scratching posts by associating them with good experiences. Play with her near the posts, or give her a treat each time she happens to come close to one. You can even rub lavender or catnip on them, to lure her in. At the very least, praise her quietly when you see her getting ready to rake her claws on one.

If you have two or more cats, be sure to have numerous scratching posts located around the home. Remember that they will be competing for and sharing territory; the ability to scratch will help define space and reduce territorial aggression that might be brewing. Notice where each cat tends to spend the most time, and locate a post there. This is in addition to communal posts located in the living room and bedrooms. If you can, pay attention to which cat favors which post; this can help you better understand the dominance dynamics of the home.

At the same time you encourage your cat to use her scratching posts, discourage her from scratching where she shouldn't. For instance, if she appears interested in the legs of your sofa, wrap aluminum foil, double-sided sticky tape, or even reversed duct tape (sticky side out) around the legs for a month or so. Do the same for any surface she thinks is "scratch-able." Eventually she'll begin to favor the posts, and leave the furniture alone.

If she still rips into furniture, you'll have to resort to a plant sprayer bottle. Wait until she just begins to go for a piece of furniture then, preferably from a hidden position or with her back to you, give her a spritz. If done correctly, she won't even know it came from you; she'll just think it was an act of the Egyptian cat goddess Bast! She will then associate the mysterious water bath with her scratching the furniture, and adjust her habits accordingly. Remember to use the sprayer bottle only as a last resort, if the tape and foil have failed to stop her.

Handling

As mentioned before, always allow your cat to set the tone of your relationship and the degree of physical contact with which she is comfortable. However, responsible cat ownership calls for regular grooming and
frequent examination of your cat, to maintain health and spot any
physical problems that might pop up. For that reason, as early in the
cat's life as possible, teach your cat to accept being handled, brushed
and examined on a daily basis. The objective is to desensitize her to
your touch, and to actually make her think that the attention is a good
thing. Bear in mind that some cats will be more accepting of handling
than others; just be more patient with a reserved cat, making sure that
sessions are positive and brief.

Start with a pat or rub on the head, followed by a treat and a kind
word. Over a period of weeks, slowly increase contact to include brief
handling of paws, tail, legs, the torso, and even her teeth, gums, ears and
privates. Consider rubbing a bit of catnip or lavender on your fingers, to
pique her curiosity. Remember to be brief and positive, to reward with
treats or play, and to stop before she objects. After a few months time
she should welcome your touch, making brushing, nail maintenance,
and a daily head-to-toe exam a breeze. Your veterinarian will be grateful
as well when the time comes for your cat's annual exam. In Secret Six:
Keep Your Cat Healthy and Safe, I'll discuss grooming in detail; for now,
just get her used to your gentle touch. And remember; let her set the
rules of engagement, resist over-stimulation, and never force the issue!

Teaching Your Cat to Play Nice

Playtime for a cat is often a thinly disguised attempt to stalk and kill
something; when she chases after a ping-pong ball or leaps for a teaser
toy, she is exercising her hunting instincts. She needs to do this; it's an
outlet, and a relief valve of sorts for all that pent-up predatory aggression. For indoor-only cats, regular play is especially important, as they
have no actual opportunities to hunt for Tweety Bird or Mickey Mouse
(thankfully).

Natural cat owners know that cats sometimes show playful aggression toward owners, and that if not dealt with, it can get out of hand. To minimize play aggression toward people or other pets, you should redirect your cat's instinctive need to stalk, grab, scratch and bite toward toys, teasers, balls and other fun objects. When allowed to focus her natural need to "kill" on play, she'll be far less likely to show inappropriate behavior toward people or other pets.

In addition to exercising her need to hunt, play will minimize boredom and the resulting misbehaviors that can ensue, such as destructive behavior, redirected aggression, or even housetraining setbacks. She'll have more to look forward to, and will associate you with fun activity. It can't help but improve your relationship!

From early on, teach your cat to play every day. Supply her with safe, non-toxic toys and teasers made from materials that won't easily tear or break apart. And don't simply put toys down and leave her; instead, participate. Toss a ball or fuzzy mouse toy for her, taunt her with a teaser wand, or lure her around the room with a feather on the end of a string. Regular play sessions will be the highlight of her day, so remember to schedule them in when you get home, or whenever your cat seems unusually frisky. For more on play and other "enrichment" activities, see Secret Five: Enrich Your Cat.

Play Gear

One of the best toys is perhaps the simplest: a ping-pong ball. Few cats can resist the chaotic bouncing and rolling, so similar to a frantic mouse or bird. The teaser wand, or a durable toy with a squeaker or bell inside also works well, as does a wind-up or battery-operated toy, or even a remote-controlled car. A trip to the pet store will reveal more toys and teasers than you can possibly cart home; just choose a few and see how she responds. Even an old standby like a balled-up wad of newspaper can work wonderfully, as can a cardboard box with newspaper and a treat or two tossed in. But one last thing: although you should always leave a few toys out for her, don't put the whole collection out at once.

Rotate them, and pull out the most desirable ones only when you are
there. That way, she won't get bored with them, and she'll learn to associate the most desirable toys with your presence and participation.

Basic Etiquette

The natural owner has the innate ability to teach his or her cat how to
behave in a civil manner, without creating undue conflict or trauma.
It's not at all like training a dog; it's an ability to persuade without
coercion, as a skilled diplomat might. Much of the "teaching" really
involves preventive measures; for example, if you never expose your
cat to potentially troublesome situations (such as snacks left on a table,
or an open container of foodstuffs), she won't get the chance to cause
trouble. By restricting your cat's access to forbidden temptations, you
prevent unwanted conditioning and unproductive behaviors.

Civility

The very least you should expect from your cat is a fundamental civility
in her relations with you and others in the home. That means no
aggressive attacks, no food or possession theft, and no destructive
behavior. A natural owner creates an atmosphere of mutual civility by
providing his or her cat with the right environment, the right food and
care, and the appropriate amount of attention, particularly with regard
to play, socialization, affection, and enrichment. Timely neutering aids
civility by minimizing marking and territorial aggression, just as an
indoor-only rule thwarts the inescapable cautiousness and apprehen-
sion common to outdoor cats. Avoiding over-aggressive handling of
your cat will also do much to prevent biting, scratching or overly fickle
behavior. Indeed, preventive behavior and respect on the part of the
owner is the single best way to ensure a civil relationship with your cat.
For truly uncivil behavior problems, refer to Part Three: The Natural
Cat Owner's Quick Guide to Solving the Most Common Cat Problems,
where the most pressing misbehavior issues will be covered.

Boundary Training

I know: the very idea of telling a cat it can't go somewhere is somewhat silly and demeaning. Yours will eventually go just about everywhere it wants to around the home without issue. But there are certain places you may not want your cat to go, and other areas which should be absolutely out-of-bounds for your cat, for safety's sake. Let's cover the main areas now.

Storage Areas

It's a good idea to teach your cat to stay out of closets and cupboards. She might damage clothing or shoes, eat potentially harmful foods, or even get into harmful chemicals. As a natural owner, use some common sense and simply keep all closets and cupboards securely closed, to prevent her from ever getting in and developing a bad habit. For those smarter cats who actually figure out how to open doors and drawers, consider installing baby-lock mechanisms, available at most hardware and box stores. Keep your bathroom door closed while gone, too, as well as the toilet lid, and keep all creams, soaps, lotions and cleaners stored away. The same goes for the kitchen; even dishwashing liquid left on the counter can be a potential health hazard.

The Garage

Probably no other area in the home has as many potentially dangerous items as the garage. Oils, anti-freeze, solvents, stains, fertilizers—the list is endless. Again, the best way to keep your cat out is to never allow her access, by keeping the doors shut. Don't take a chance though; still store all potential toxins away behind secured cupboards and in locked drawers. And remember: simply locating them up high on a shelf won't work for Kitty as it might with Fido.

If your cat is allowed outdoors, be aware of her trying to enter the garage from the outside, when the door is up. And beware of her sneaking into the engine compartment of your garaged vehicle, where she could be torn to ribbons in the morning when you start up.

Off-Limits Areas

If there are rooms you want her to stay out of, keep the doors closed. Simple, right? Not if you have kids, who often leave doors open all over the home. Decide on a strategy in a family meeting, and stick to it! The first time one of your kids finds a favorite sweater chewed to smithereens, the door-closing lesson will be learned!

If certain communal, accessible areas of the home are to be off-limits to your cat, you'll have to use the sticky tape/foil method to discourage her. Tops of fine pieces of furniture, areas where family portraits or photos are kept, collections of fragile trinkets—wherever she isn't invited will need your creative, consistent attention, and perhaps an occasional visit from the plant sprayer fairy.

Some owners go so far as to use static electrical devices in and around forbidden areas. These contain a harmless charge of static electricity (similar to one you might get touching your car door). When the cat steps on the mat it gets the tiny shock, discouraging further forays into the area. Though not harmful, I have never found this type of device to be necessary. The combination of prevention and the rare squirt from a sprayer is all you really need, in my opinion.

Nighttime Etiquette

Most owners don't mind at all when cats choose to sleep with them at night. Having a cuddly furball under the covers can actually be fun, especially on cold nights! Unlike dogs, who can develop dominance issues if allowed to sleep in their owners' beds, cats have no such issues. The only problem can occur due to the cat's somewhat nocturnal nature; they can be little balls of energy at three in the morning, just when we should be snoring away.

If that becomes a problem for you, you can try a number of things. First, see to it that your cat gets more exercise during the day, by playing with her several times and by providing her with toys to play with while you are gone. Next, consider feeding her a bit later in the day; the digestive process might slow her down enough for you to get a good night's sleep. Or, simply banish her from the bedroom altogether. This works better if you deny her access from the very start; if she's used to it, she will most likely complain vocally for a time, and may even take to scratching at the door. Most cats will give up after a few nights, but for those who do not, here is a novel solution that, though not at all harmful, will annoy her a bit. Take a radio or vacuum cleaner and position it in front of your closed bedroom door. Thread the power cord under the door into your bedroom, then plug it into a switch box, available at any hardware or retail superstore; the switch box will have an "in" outlet, a cord to plug into a wall outlet, and an on/off switch. After plugging in the appliance, plug the switch box into an outlet near your bed and locate the switch within your reach. Now turn the switch to the "off" position while turning the power button on the appliance on.

If your cat comes to the bedroom door and starts scratching and yowling incessantly, simply turn the switch on for a few seconds, triggering loud music or the vacuum cleaner. Then turn it off and see what happens. Odds are only a few tries will cure her of the annoying habit. Though a bit dramatic, it won't hurt her in the least, and will allow you to get a good night's sleep!

Riding in the Car

Unlike dogs, there are far fewer reasons for your cat to go for regular rides in the car. Most cats are homebodies, and prefer not to travel anywhere, especially by car, a silly contraption that travels too fast and far from home. Though some owners condition their cats from kittenhood to go for rides (nothing wrong with that), most simply keep their felines home when they venture forth by car.

Nevertheless, several times per year you may need to transport your cat by car. Whether it's a trip to the veterinarian, to a friend's home for cat-sitting duties, or even relocation to another neighborhood, your cat may need a ride every now and then. Natural owners know that simply tossing the cat into the car for a harrowing jaunt across town isn't the way to prepare her for such an ordeal. Instead, a conditioning process combined with the right equipment is the better way to go.

The most common reason for transporting a cat is, of course, for an annual trip to the veterinarian. Because of the importance of this, you need to make sure your cat will be able to accept short rides without undue anxiety. Also, cats who rarely travel by car can become carsick, an unpleasant experience for both cat and owner.

Here's what to do. First, from as early on in the cat's life as possible, get her used to short stints in a travel carrier; available from your local pet store. You can opt for either a soft-sided or hard-sided carrier. The soft carriers are lighter and more easily storable, whereas the hard ones are more durable, and a bit easier to clean. Soft carriers work better on a plane, as they will more easily mold to the available under-seat space than will hard versions. Hard carriers will resist staining better though, and will hold up better to chewer kitties. Whichever you choose, be sure it has adequate ventilation, is easily cleaned, and that its flooring is rigid enough to prevent excess flexing, which might impart a feeling of insecurity to your cat.

Many owners only use the carrier when taking their cats to the veterinarian. This almost certainly guarantees that your cat will head for the hills whenever she sees it. To avoid this, you need to associate the carrier with happy thoughts. When you purchase a carrier, consider leaving it out for her to investigate; toss a treat into it, or rub the insides with a bit of catnip, lavender, or a dot of meat-flavored baby food. Placing a favorite toy inside will also help get her to investigate the interior. You can even feed her in the carrier if she is willing; whatever works.

Once she will enter the carrier without fear, move it around the home, to generalize the behavior. Then, while she is inside, casually close the door for a minute, then open it. The goal is to be able to get her comfortable with being in the carrier for fifteen minutes or so without anxiety.

After accomplishing this, it's time to pick up the carrier and move it around the home, with her in it. Start out with short moves, and gradually extend the time you carry her until she can tolerate being moved all about the home. Remember to always reward her with whatever she likes afterwards.

Then, with her in the carrier, take her out to the car. Place the carrier on a seat rather than the floor or the storage area in the back, as the seat padding will dampen vibrations better, reducing her stress. After a minute or two, take her back inside and reward her with treats and praise, or a play session. Gradually lengthen the time she is in the car, until fifteen minutes is not a problem.

Then it's time to go for a short ride down the block and back. Gradually lengthen the ride time until you can make fifteen minutes without any stress-related issues. Once she can tolerate this, schedule a weekly trip around the block, to desensitize her to the experience.

Some cats will take to it quickly, while others will object; if your cat simply cannot get comfortable going for rides in the carrier, accept it and know that taking her for rides will be a bit stressful for all parties. At the very least though, remember to always leave the carrier out somewhere in the home to desensitize her to it. Leave the door open; she'll quickly accept it as one of many interesting playthings in the home, and won't necessarily consider it as a harbinger of movable anxiety.

The Power of Vocabulary

Intelligence is defined not only by the innate computing power of an animal's brain, but by the ability of that brain to store information and then correlate it. The more available information an animal can store, the more associations can be made, and the wider the range of under-standing.

You can increase your cat's IQ by enlarging her vocabulary. By conditioning her to associate a word with an action or circumstance, you can literally make her smarter. And who wouldn't want a smarter cat? It's exciting to watch a cat respond to a word or hand sign, and know that she is associating an abstract term with an action.

For instance, if you say *"eat?"* each time you prepare to feed her, she will quickly learn what the word means, and come running when you use it. The same can apply to any other activities she enjoys or items she covets. Say *"play?"* before pulling out a toy and she'll soon learn what it means; the same goes for *"treat,"* or even *"water"* when she's thirsty. Just try to always associate a word or hand sign with something she likes, and you'll soon have her responding to it.

The simplest word she should learn is her name. If you use it often enough, she'll come to associate it with herself, or at least with her presence with you. Say it whenever you come home, or when you pet her; soon she'll understand it to be exclusive to her. Another fundamental word is of course *"good,"* used to shape the behaviors you like. Say *"good"* when she is being sweet, then quickly match it with a treat or pet on the head, to teach her that the word means she's doing the right thing. It sounds simple, but it does teach her, and stimulate her brain.

You can also teach her words that mediate behavior, such as *"off"* or *"no."* Though it's better to teach your cat what you want her to do (and then reinforce that behavior with attention and treats), you can use mild negative reinforcement to stop a behavior such as climbing the drapes or scratching the sofa; a spray from a plant sprayer bottle or a shake of a can with a few pebbles inside is usually the most you ever need. Pairing these actions with the word *"no"* will eventually teach her that the word means *"stop what you are doing."* Soon all you'll need to do is say *"no"* and she will get the message, without the water or can noise.

Trick Training

Cats are by no means dogs, and as such need not perform silly behaviors for their owners. But teaching your cat to do fun behaviors can be a fine way to build her IQ, and strengthen her bond with you. It's a no-stress activity, as she need not do it. Working on a specific trick will, if done correctly, give her something to look forward to, build confidence, and help relieve boredom. And, for those who think that it's an affront to a cat's dignity to learn tricks, realize that a cat will *never* do anything it does not want to do; if she gets bored or annoyed, she'll just walk away. She is a master of self-interest; only if you make it fun and worthwhile will she respond.

Some cats will be better performers than others. If your cat is outgoing and confident, she'll most likely do well. But if she is the timid type, she might not respond, and may actually object to any kind of structured learning experience. If she isn't into it, don't push it; but if she is the friendly, curious type, by all means give it a go.

To get your cat to perform, you'll have to offer her something she wants. That's usually going to be food. Choose a treat that she'll be crazy for, like bits of cheese or tuna instead of her normal food. That way she'll be more likely to pay attention. Or, use a favorite toy to inspire her. Also, be sure to make your training session short and sweet so she remains interested. Make sure you are in a quiet room with no distractions, to ensure focus and prevent any chance of nervousness. Never *require* her to do anything, and avoid *any* negative reinforcement. After all, she is a cat, not a poodle! Also, consider teaching her while she is atop a table instead of down on the floor; this will put her at eye-level with you, and help raise her confidence level.

Age

The younger your cat is, the more likely she will be able to learn and perform new behaviors such as tricks. A six-month-old will be much more capable of performing than will a six-year-old. It's just the way all animals are; it even applies to humans. Don't quit on the older cat, though. All cats are capable, given enough time. The trick training will just take little bit longer.

Five Tricks You Can Teach Your Cat

Here are five behaviors your cat can learn to perform on command (or, more correctly, *on request*). Remember to be patient and brief, and to always associate a word with the behavior.

Sit

First, make sure your cat is hungry! Place her atop a table in front of you, in a standing position. If she won't stand, pet her rump; this usually makes cats stand. Now hold a bit of cheese or tuna right near her nose and let her get a whiff. As soon as she gets interested, slowly move the treat up and back slightly, from her nose to a point between her ears. She should eagerly follow it up with her nose. As you move the treat, say *"Kitty, Sit."* This will take some practice; hold it too close and she'll just try to eat it, while keeping it too far away will cause her to lose interest. Raising it too high above her head will cause her to stand up on her two hind legs.

If all goes well she will follow the path of the offered treat and naturally sit. If she does, immediately give her the treat and say *"Good Sit!"* Once you learn how to manipulate the treat properly, she should sit. Give it three or four tries; if she doesn't get it, try again later.

Once you get her to sit, keep working it two or three times each day for very brief sessions. Your goal should be for her to associate the word with the action. Be sure to always reward her with something tasty!

Kiss

I hope you don't mind getting a little messy! Teaching your cat to kiss your cheek will require you to dab a bit of tasty food on a friend's face, so if you can't find a volunteer, you can pass on this one. But it's a fun one to teach, so why not give it a try?

To teach "Kiss," you'll need to use a treat that will adhere to a person's cheek (yuck!). Tuna or cheese won't do; try cream cheese, or meat-flavored baby food. First, place her on a table in front of a helper, who is sitting with his or her face about a foot away from the cat. The preferred treat should already be on the lucky person's cheek. Now, let the cat get up close to your helper's cheek. The objective is to have her notice the cheek treat and begin licking at it. The helper may have to maneuver his or her face accordingly.

As soon as the cat attempts to lick, say *"Fluffy, Kiss!"* If she does, say *"Good Kiss!"* and then quickly offer her a piece of tuna or cheese as a reward. Practice this two or three times each day until she will reliably "kiss" your helper's cheek.

Now, begin to slowly reduce the amount of goo you put on your poor helper's cheek, until after a week or so there is barely a hint of it. Also, slowly increase the distance between the cat and your helper, until after a week or so the starting distance is four to six feet, or the lengthwise distance of a tabletop. Always reward her with a super treat each time she kisses.

Eventually you should be able to say *"Fluffy, Kiss!"* and have her kiss your own cheek. Just remember to always reward and praise her. Also, have others your cat likes do the same, to generalize the trick.

Spin

The behavior you want is simple: get your cat to spin around in a circle. Start the trick with your cat in front of you, on the floor, with you kneeling down in front of her. Show her a treat in your right hand, hold it near her nose, then slowly lure her around in a circle while saying *"Spin."* Be sure to hold the treat near her nose. If she follows the treat, give her the treat. Even if she only follows it for a quarter turn, still reward and praise her!

Continue trying to get her to spin all the way around. If you can only get a partial turn, though, don't fret. Stop, then repeat in a half hour or so. Eventually you will get her to spin all the way around.

Work this trick each day, slowly increasing the speed of the spin. The rounded hand action you use to bait the cat around eventually becomes the hand signal for "Spin." As you begin to get farther from your cat, continue to use the same hand action, but reduce the size of the circle you make. The goal is to get her to spin without you having to lead her all the way around with a treat. You should eventually be able to give the hand signal or spoken command from five feet away and have your cat spin around. Reward and praise when she succeeds! After teaching "Spin" in one direction, teach her to do it in the opposite direction, using your other hand to signal.

Down

Teaching "Down" will necessitate patience on your part, as it isn't as easy as the others. Cats do not necessarily like being in a "Down" position, since to her it is being in a submissive, vulnerable posture. However, if your cat is confident and outgoing, it shouldn't be too hard.

Start your cat in a sitting position on a table, as close to the edge as possible, so that when she does lie down, her nose will be just off the table. Now hold a treat close to her nose. Move the treat straight down until it is slightly below the edge of the table. As you do, say *"Down."* She will hopefully follow the treat down, and go into a crouching pose.

When the cat crouches, help her into a complete down position by softly pushing on her shoulders. When she extends her front paws out, give her the treat and lots of praise.

Take your time at this stage; a week or more is not unusual. If your cat doesn't like to be handled, you may have to opt for the crouching position, instead of the complete "Down."

You may have to rest your hand on your cat's shoulders at first, to keep her in the position. If you trick her into thinking that you are petting her, it will usually work out well. When done working this (or any) trick, happily say *"Okay!"* This releases the cat from training session.

Shake

Though not a difficult trick to teach, you should know that many cats do not like having their feet manipulated or held for lengthy periods. So, when teaching "Shake," take care not to manhandle your cat's feet. If the cat wants to quit, let her. Be sure you know that your cat won't mind having her feet handled before working on this trick.

Start with your cat sitting near the edge of a table. Then say *"Shake,"* while at the same time using your right hand to softly lift her paw. As you shake her paw, immediately give her a treat. Then praise her and let go.

Work this part of the trick five times a day for a few days before continuing on. By then, she should have grasped that when you lift her paw, she gets a treat.

Once she gets this stage, it's time to move on. Reach out as if to grab her paw, only this time don't touch it. Say *"Shake,"* then move your hand close to the cat's foot. Hopefully, your cat will raise her paw all on her own, in anticipation. If she does, take the paw then reward and praise mightily! Even if she just barely moves her paw on her own, reward.

If your cat won't offer her paw, try tapping on the back of her wrist while repeating *"Shake."* This should help persuade her to offer her paw. When she finally does, take the paw, reward and praise. Reaching your hand out ultimately becomes the hand signal for the trick.

Once your cat is consistently offering her paw, try teaching her to raise the other. You can use a different command, such as *"Wave,"* instead of *"Shake."* Reaching with your left hand becomes the hand signal for the cat to offer her other paw.

Other Teaching Opportunities

Whenever you can, try to foster an exploratory nature in your cat. Rotate her toys so she always has the chance to investigate something new and fun. Challenge her courage and intellect by randomly introducing subtle changes, such as a small ramp leading up to the first shelf of a bookcase, with a sprig of catnip at the top. Teach her to walk on the top sill of a door. Get her to fetch a ball or mouse toy. Make a tunnel out of a cardboard box and lure her through with a treat or teaser. Whatever stimulates her brain will build confidence and boost her ability to deal with the unexpected. Remember: she is a predator, with a savvy brain that needs to be challenged!

Enrich Your Cat's Environment

For decades, zoos across the globe housed their animals in spartan cages that bore little or no resemblance to the animals' natural habitats. Lions, tigers, bears, wolves, apes—all led a barren, boring existence behind bars, like convicted prisoners doomed to be gawked at year after year by generations of visitors.

Big cats like lions, tigers and leopards suffered terribly; denied an outlet for their predatory natures, keen senses and intellects, they languished into depression and poor health. Their chronic boredom caused anorexia, aggression and antisocial behavior, and even led to low libido and poor parenting skills. Denied any significant environmental or behavioral stimuli, they withered psychologically, and often died prematurely.

Zoo Enrichment

Today's zookeepers don't let that happen. Trained to keep their charges happy and healthy, they construct diverse, stimulating habitats for the animals, custom-tailored to the particular species' natural ecosystem and filled with appealing sights, sounds, tastes and smells. In addition to the customized environment, the animals are motivated to practice behaviors they might normally demonstrate in the wild, such as tracking, chasing, procuring food, and even mating and parenting. Captive polar bears hunt in cold water ponds stocked with trout; zoo leopards climb trees to reach hidden carcasses; wolves follow a scent

trail of dripped fat or lavender to a cache of frozen chickens; chim-
panzees use twigs to probe zoo-provided termite nests—the list of
enrichments is long. These help make the animals feel comfortable with
their captivity, and arouse natural instincts necessary for their psychological and physiological well being. Compared to sixty years ago, zoo
animals have it made.

Your Cat's Home Is Boring!

Your cat deserves at least the same level of stimulation and enrichment
as those zoo animals. Unfortunately, the typical domestic cat spends her
day in a home nearly as devoid of enrichment as zoos from the fifties.
Her instincts to hunt, explore, play and interact are rarely employed;
instead, she wanders the home, eats, sleeps, stares out the window, eats,
sleeps, waits. It is a boring existence, with little resemblance to a cat's
natural environment. With her senses and brain rarely engaged, she
becomes as listless and strained as an inmate in solitary confinement.
An under-stimulated cat can obsess on food, become destructive or
aggressive, lose litter box skills, become hyper-vocal, or even develop
psychosomatic disorders such as excessive grooming or scratching.
Bored cats may even try to escape the home in an effort to find
something fun to do.

Lions Are Never Bored

In the wild, felines lead a challenging, diverse lifestyle. They hunt,
mate, play, raise young, maintain territory and defend themselves from
predators and other competing felines. There is not a waking moment
wasted. This multifaceted existence ensures that the feline's mind and
body remains stimulated all of the time, guaranteeing good physical
and psychological health. Lions and tigers rarely get bored, overweight,
depressed or self-destructive, and are rarely needlessly aggressive toward
others of their own kind. They remain alert and clever because that is
what their environment demands of them.

Not so for the domestic cat. Most do not hunt, mate, raise young, or participate in complex territorial disputes. They have minuscule territories, few distractions, and extremely limited routines. Though safe from the dangers of the wild, our cats rarely get to sample nature's abundant and developmentally vital stimuli. They are not required to use their natural gifts, and as such tend to get bored to tears.

The Importance of Enrichment

If zookeepers can enrich the lives of captive lions and tigers, you can certainly do the same for your domestic kitty. By providing her with captivating distractions and by creating a diverse, stimulating home setting, you'll guarantee her plenty of intellectual and physical diversions while you are gone. Her senses will be engaged, as will her predatory instincts, which she needs to express in order to be truly content. By filling her world with cat-friendly stimuli, you will be enriching her environment, and appealing to her craving to be a cat and not a doormat. She'll be happier, fitter, and better adjusted to life with you.

Natural cat owners always create and maintain a stimulating home environment for their cats, filled with environmental and behavioral enrichments. Able to empathize with his or her cat's yearning for purpose and exploration, the "natural" turns his or her home into a stimulating place that appeals to the cat's curious nature.

Enrichments

You needn't be a zoologist or scientist to enrich your cat's home environment. All that's needed is imagination, some toys and treats, and a variety of items found either in the home or the pet store. If done consistently, your cat's species-specific behavior will be stimulated, making her happier and better adjusted to her home.

The enrichments are broken down into two categories: *environmental* and *behavioral*. Environmental enrichments include any unique objects or individuals introduced into your cat's environment, or changes made to the home territory. Each of your cat's five senses will be stimulated, as will her prey and territorial drives. Behavioral enrichments include any unique stimulating activities you involve your cat in, such as play, mock hunting, or even "hide-and-seek" games.

Environmental Enrichments

You can make your cat's home "territory" a more enriching place to live simply by introducing fun, stimulating items and changes for your cat to experience. For instance, whenever I leave a cat alone in the home, I supply fun distractions designed to stimulate one or more of her senses. Let me provide you with a selection of environmental enrichments you can use, categorized by your pet's senses:

Visual Enrichments

Compared to her olfactory and auditory abilities, your cat's vision isn't her sharpest sense. Nevertheless, visual variations to the home can be a great way to stimulate her imagination. I'm not including toys and chews here, as they fall under taste or prey-drive enrichments. Some good visual enrichments include:

> **Leave the television tuned to a station with pet programming. Keep the sound just loud enough for your cat to hear. You can even rent a pet-themed DVD or videotape and play it for her while you are gone!**

> **Install several mirrors around the home, mounted at cat height. Most cats think it's another cat, making for some interesting meetings. Remove the mirrors if she becomes destructive or aggressive.**

> **Hang a few large mobiles about the home, in a place she cannot reach. Attach one to a slow-moving ceiling fan if you have one. Color matters less than design; feel free to use photos of pets, or even yourself.**

> **Move a piece of furniture in one room. Even a subtle shift of position can pique your cat's curiosity. The purchase of new**

furniture will also stimulate her interest. Just don't overdo it, as a dramatic change might stress her out.

Purchase real or artificial plants and place them about the home. If she digs in the dirt or tries to eat them, relocate them up high, or cover the soil with either rocks or attachable plastic covers available at garden centers. Also, be sure to avoid toxic houseplants such as aloe vera, poinsettia, fern, lily, dieffenbachia, philodendron, and agave. (Note: This is a partial list only; for a more complete list, please refer to "How the Home Set-up Affects Health" in Secret Six.)

Stock a ten-gallon aquarium with active fish and place it in sight but out of your cat's reach. Make sure it is lighted, and securely covered. She should find it amusing.

Leave a curtain or two partially open, to allow your cat something of a view.

Vary the lighting in the home while you are gone. Having certain lights go on and off automatically by means of a timer will get her thinking.

Move her food dish or water bowl, or leave safe, random objects scattered about.

Olfactory Enrichments

Your cat's sense of smell is keen; to take advantage of this, provide her with olfactory enrichments in and around the home. These can include the following:

Leave trace amounts of lavender oil, cinnamon, or allspice about the home. Consider leaving a trail of one of these, leading to a rewarding treat or toy.

Hide a few bouillon cubes about the home; the aroma will get your cat searching. The same can be done with minute amounts of sprinkled instant soup mix. Avoid using too much of either though, as their sodium content can be somewhat high.

Place a freshly cut evergreen bough in a vase up high; its fresh, powerful aroma will make your cat think it's hiking in the woods!

Hide catnip somewhere in the home. Try placing it beneath an area rug, or inside a hard rubber toy; your cat will spend lots of time trying to get at the aromatic treasure. You can also stuff a crochet ball with catnip and leave it for her.

Place some coffee grounds inside a paper bag and leave it just out of your cat's reach. She'll be craving a cup of java when you get home.

Dab vanilla extract onto bits of paper and hide them. Like the lavender and spices, she'll seek them out.

Rub a piece of aromatic cheese onto various areas in the home, such as windowsills, or underneath a table. She'll go bananas looking for it.

Hide hairs from another pet in random places. Your cat will wonder where the interloper is; this healthy "stressor" will stimulate her. You can do the same with feathers or even a friend's hair.

Auditory Enrichments

Cats have better hearing than we do, especially in the higher ranges. In addition, their multi-directional ears "funnel" sound, helping them locate prey. You can stimulate your cat's auditory world in these ways:

In a closed room, leave a radio on tuned to classical music or talk radio. Your cat will think that someone is home. You can also set your clock radio alarm to go off randomly while you are gone, tuned to talk radio or classical. Avoid harsh music, though, as this can upset some cats.

Purchase a thirty-second-long endless-loop audio tape (the type used in older answering machines). Record yourself saying something (*"Hi, Kitty; are you being a good girl?"*); then, when you are ready to leave the home, place the tape into a tape player located in a closed room, push play, then leave. Your five- to ten-second message will play repeatedly while you are gone. You can record other sounds as well; try the voice of another friendly person, birds chirping, or even a cat meowing!

Purchase a "sounds of nature" tape or CD and play it at low volume for your cat while you are gone.

Call home while gone and leave an audible message for your kitty. You can also use walkie-talkies to amuse her; set one in the living room, then take the other outside and talk to her from down the street!

Tactile Enrichments

Changes in how the home environment feels to your cat will keep her on her toes. These can include the following:

Randomly place area rugs of varying pile about the home. Rotate their position every few days. These will stimulate her visually and tactilely. Try combining olfactory enrichment by dabbing them with lavender oil or sprinkling one with a bit of allspice or cinnamon.

Vary slightly the temperature of your home each day. The subtle changes will be noticed and appraised by your cat.

Purchase a kitty condo or cat tree for your pet and set it up in the living room. These multi-leveled, carpeted constructs will provide your cat with hours of fun, and even a place to rest. Make sure whatever you buy measures at least four or five feet in height, as cats like to perch up high. Kitty condos with built-in box enclosures are ideal.

On warm days, turn on a fan. The breeze will be noticed and appreciated by your cat. Just be sure to keep the fan and its power cord out of reach. An overhead fan works best.

Leave an ice cube in her water dish. It's surprising texture and temperature will engross her.

Give your cat massages. The tactile experience will please her, and desensitize her to being handled. Try this only with cats who do not fear handling; timid cats might not tolerate it for very long.

Edible Enrichments

Clever dispersal of edibles around the home can stimulate one of your cat's most fundamental drives. Used by zookeepers to arouse the prey drive and compel cats to hunt, edible enrichments put cats into problem-solving mode.

Edible enrichments you can try on your cat include:

Move your cat's food and water dish, to make her search for her meal. Move them only a small distance at first, then gradually relocate them to different rooms or floors of the home. You can also elevate them, or place the food in three or four bowls instead of one. Let her search without help at first; only hint at the food's location if she fails to locate it after ten minutes. Use this enrichment only occasionally, to make the search worthwhile and challenging. If she reacts poorly to this, move the water and food dishes back to their original location.

Vary slightly the amounts of food you feed your cat. One day give her three-quarters the normal amount; the next day give her a quarter more. Avoid feeding excessive amounts though, as this can affect litter box habits.

Supplement your cat's diet with raw or partially cooked meats on a random schedule. Grind up and serve a portion of a chicken neck, or give her a small slice of fresh liver. Avoid bones, except for those in ground chicken necks. Never feed cooked bones, as they splinter. Though a cat's digestive tract is designed to process raw food, consider microwaving raw meats for thirty seconds or blanching in boiling water for the same length of time, to kill surface bacteria. For more on a raw food diet, see the section titled Homemade Cat Food in Secret Six.

Hide treats about the home, in corners, on stairs, under throw rugs—wherever she's allowed to be. Once she gets into search mode, reduce the number of treats and increase the level of difficulty in finding them. Ideally she will use her sense of smell more than vision to locate them. You can even leave a trail of treat bits that lead to a bigger treat, or to her relocated dinner dish.

Leave a few durable, veterinarian-approved cat toys about the home. She'll play with them while you are gone. Provide toys that your cat cannot destroy, unless you are there to supervise. Also rotate toys from day to day to keep her interested. Don't use too many at once, or she will become bored.

Most cats like chewing on wheat grass, so leave a small pot of it out somewhere for your cat to access. You can either buy it at your pet store, or purchase some grass seed and grow your own! This will also help dissuade her from chewing on your houseplants.

Try smearing a small amount of canned food inside a hard rubber ball toy and leaving it on the floor for her. She will spend lots of time trying to get at the goodies.

Leave a raw, uncracked quail or pigeon egg in her food bowl. She'll be puzzled at first, but will quickly solve the delicious puzzle. Don't worry about the raw egg; her digestive system is designed to deal with it. Chicken eggs might work for some big cats, but are usually too large for the average cat to break open. Find quail or pigeon eggs at any Asian market.

Freeze small pieces of meat inside meat broth ice cubes and leave them in her food dish. She'll lick and crunch the cubes to get at the prize.

Get a large cardboard box, fill it with crumpled newspaper, and drop a few aromatic treats into it. Leave the open box out in the living room for the cat to investigate.

Social Enrichments around the Home

Cats differ greatly in their desire for socialization, especially with other pets. Some want nothing to do with people from outside the home, while others love the attention. Generally, most cats won't appreciate visits from strange cats or dogs, so think about avoiding this, unless you have a cat who likes that sort of thing. But regarding people, if she seems to appreciate the occasional visit from a cat-savvy human, go ahead and give it a try.

For confident cats, enrichments around the home should include social visits. Natural cat owners know this, and as such make sure that their cats have contact with calm cat lovers who know to let the cat set the tone of the visit. That means petting only when the cat happily makes herself available for it. And, when the cat decides she's had enough, the visitor accepts this and doesn't force the pet to endure any more attention. This applies especially to children, who must be taught to be gentle, calm and tolerant. Never let a child chase a cat around the home!

The following social enrichments will, if introduced slowly and to a confident cat, work well. Try some or all!

Pay unexpected visits home during the day. Try entering through the back door sometimes, if you have one. If you have time, play with her for a few minutes. She'll love the surprise!

Schedule visits to your home by trusted friends. Choose only people your cat trusts, with you present. At first have them sit passively in the living room; they can read a book, or sip some tea. Often just having them there is enough to stimulate your cat. Do not try this if your cat shows anxiety over others coming into your home. They can toss a few treats to her also, if she seems willing.

Have select, well-behaved, cat-savvy children over the age of twelve visit. Doing so will help teach your cat to trust capable young persons. Again, skip this one if your cat dislikes strangers. If your cat likes treats, have the child toss a few down to her.

If (and only if) your cat seems very open to the presence ofother pets, consider bringing a kitten into the home for a short visit. Keep the kitten in a carrier and simply let them sniff each other through the mesh door. Only use a kitten who is already used to the presence of other cats, and keep the visit short. If your cat appears happy about the meeting, increase the visit duration. At some point, you can consider allowing the kitten out of the carrier to interact with your cat. Try this in a small room with the door closed, and no food or toys present. If your cat seems happy with this, you might then consider adopting a new kitten. Do not try this with an adult cat visitor, as the social dynamics will be more complicated; odds are your cat won't appreciate having another adult cat in her territory. Kittens are much less of a territorial threat, however.

Behavioral Enrichments

Any stimulating activities your cat participates in are considered behavioral enrichments. Rather than just altering your cat's home environment and then allowing her to react, behavioral enrichments require your cat to *actively take part*. These activities tap into your cat's need to play, explore, stalk, and catch.

The following are some excellent behavioral enrichments you can undertake with your cat. Give some a try; your cat may love the added activity.

Prey-driven Enrichments

When a cat chases a mouse toy or feather teaser, she is really showing her predatory drive to capture and covet prey. Remember, your kitty's heart is much closer to the wild than you may realize!

The feline prey drive, though closely related to the food drive, adds the passion of the hunt; it's "process" rather than "product" that truly excites the cat. That's why I have separated edible enrichments from prey-driven ones; the former involve simple eating, the latter chasing, which is more meaningful from the cat's perspective. Try the following:

> **Many cats will fetch a ball or toy, or at the very least run after a thrown object and pounce on it. This will tap into her desire to chase, catch, and even bring "prey" back to you, her "mother." Try it with a stuffed mouse, or a ping-pong ball.**

> **Some cats go bonkers for the light trail of a flashlight or laser pen. The erratic course of the bright point of light can send many cats into hyper-chase mode; watching them go nuts trying to capture the phantom can get comical! When using a laser pen, be sure not to shine the beam into anyone's eyes, as it can cause injury.**

> **Turning on a battery-operated, wind-up, or remote-controlled toy around the home for your cat to chase can be a fun way to stimulate her prey drive. Pet shops and mainstream toy**

stores often sell animated toys; try a few out and see how your cat reacts to them. Be sure not to leave her alone with one, though, as she might destroy or eat the toy. Another option is to use a toy that talks, barks, or meows!

Some cats respond to a teaser toy waved in their direction. A dangled fake mouse dabbed with lavender oil or beef broth also can work. As with any toy, don't let your cat have it for too long, as she may destroy or eat it. This type of enrichment works particularly well with outgoing cats.

Like the remote-controlled toys, most cats will go nuts for a small train set. Set it up in a corner of the living room and turn it on twice each day. Odds are she will pounce on the choo-choo right away.

Keep Your Cat Healthy and Safe

Caring, Naturally

Perhaps the most significant indicator of whether or not someone is a natural cat owner is the ability to keep one's cat fit and protected. Natural cat owners invariably have their cats for a very long time; it's not unusual to see seventeen- or eighteen-year-old felines softly walking about their homes. They take good care of their pets, not only from a preventive health perspective, but in terms of how safe the home environment is, how nutritious the cat's diet is, how expertly the cat is supervised—all aspects of a cat's well-being. Confused cat owners, though just as well-meaning , may not understand what their roles are with regard to keeping their cats safe, and in tip-top shape. Allowing cats to wander the streets, providing them with poor-quality food, not cat-proofing the home environment, ignoring the veterinarian until crisis strikes—these are indicators of an owner who does not have the innate ability to know what is good for a cat.

To be a natural cat owner, you need to express your feline "maternal" instincts, and take good care of your furry friend. Remember, according to Secret Three: Create a Parental Partnership, you are "big momma" in your cat's eyes; a major part of that title involves doing your best to protect your pet in the most natural, assertive way possible. It means having a heightened feline sense about the safety of the surroundings, and toward any factors that contribute to your cat's health.

Cats at Risk

Just what can go wrong with a cat? Plenty! Your feline can develop potentially fatal diseases. A vehicle, or another animal, can injure her. She can develop illness from malnutrition. She can become obese or anorexic, or develop an allergic reaction. She might even be hurt by something inside your own home, such as a power cord, spilled solvent, or toxic plant.

Of the many dangers threatening your domestic kitty, the lion's share of them can be avoided simply by being a responsible owner who, by utilizing effective feline empathy, can elude disaster before it ever becomes an issue. For example, perhaps the best way to shorten your cat's life is to allow her to wander the neighborhood. This may work in rural areas, but in urban or suburban locales it's just asking for trouble. The risk of a vehicle hitting your cat; or a dog, raccoon, coyote or other cat injuring or killing her is just too great, no matter what the "free roaming" advocates say. Infectious disease, poisoning or loss of your opportunistic cat to another cat-loving home are also common, avoidable risks.

Even the most well-meaning owners can put their cats at risk. Poor nutrition, for example, is one of the leading causes of poor health, especially in middle-aged or elderly cats. Feeding a cat poor-quality food for years can encourage undesirable metabolic processes, slowly damage internal organs and other systems, trigger allergic reactions, and even adversely affect behavior. Even inadequate grooming on the part of an owner can negatively affect a cat, especially with longhaired breeds, and with outdoor cats, whose self-grooming habits cannot keep up with the gritty environment. Truly, without a caring natural cat owner at the helm, health calamities can make life for a cat miserable.

KEEP ALERT TO CHANGES IN YOUR CAT'S BEHAVIOR. THEY ARE OFTEN YOUR FIRST INDICATION OF A HEALTH PROBLEM.

Veterinary Support:
The Essential Partnership

The most important person in your cat's life besides you is your veterinarian. Good veterinarians don't just vaccinate or treat existing symptoms; they look for subtle signs of oncoming illness or disease that, if caught early on, can be managed or eliminated. Good vets practice preventive health care, making sure all sensible vaccinations are given, and that your cat's diet contains the right nutrients. They clean teeth, eliminate parasites, and even examine coat and skin for signs of possible illness.

Veterinarians can help with behavioral issues, particularly those caused by a medical problem. They can suggest solutions to litter box setbacks, and even counsel you on grooming.

Your vet will be there in times of emergency. Should an accident or urgent medical situation require life-saving treatment or surgery, he or she can save the day.

When alerted to a problem, the natural owner understands the vital role a veterinarian plays in the health of his or her pet. As a natural owner, never hesitate to bring your veterinarian in on any problem, however small it may seem.

Confused owners wait until serious symptoms surface before scheduling a visit. Still others make an appointment only when vaccinations are due, or when infestations make home life insufferable. They go to their own doctors once each year for a preventive check-up; why deny their cats the same courtesy?

At your cat's yearly exam, your vet will weigh her, give her a complete physical exam, and check vital signs. He or she will also probably perform several tests, including:

Blood test, to check for:
Red and white cell count, indicative of possible anemia or infection

Hemoglobin assessment, to determine if enough oxygen is being delivered to the cells

Platelet count, to access clotting ability

Blood glucose, indicative of diabetes (excess glucose) or hypoglycemia (insufficient glucose)

Excess amounts of waste materials and other substances indicative of liver or kidney failure

Urinalysis, to check for:
Blood in the urine, indicative of infection, or bladder or kidney disease

Excess sugar, a possible sign of diabetes

Excess proteins, a sign of possible organ disease

Urine concentration, an indicator of dehydration

Any infection or infestation

Fecal test, to check for:
Parasitic infection

Gastrointestinal disease

Any needed vaccinations will be given, as well as treatments such as flea-and-tick preventive or de-worming medication. If necessary, X-rays or ultrasound can diagnose broken bones or other internal problems. Even your cat's teeth and gums will be examined for problems.

If all goes well, your cat will get a clean bill of health. If not, you're right where you'll need to be for the best help.

When to Take Your Cat to the Veterinarian

Be aware of your cat's appearance and behavior. Unusual symptoms should prompt you to see your veterinarian; these include:

Coughing or sneezing

Shivering, drooling, panting or excess vocalization

Excess scratching

Altered sleep patterns, or hiding

Change in appetite, thirst or elimination habits

Persistent head shaking

Lethargy or hyperactivity

Lameness

Greasy coat or hair loss

Uncharacteristic aggression

Excess discharges

Rashes or sores

Uncharacteristic odor

Pale gums

Discomfort to the touch

Loss of balance

If you have a veterinarian you trust, stick with him or her. But if you are in the market for a new veterinarian for your cat, consider one who deals exclusively with cats. These professionals focus only on the feline condition, and as such might be better informed on the latest feline diseases and trends, and better attuned to symptoms and situations unique to a cat. The office will be suited specifically to cats, not only with regard to the proper equipment and personnel, but to the curious absence of huge barking dogs, who might stress your cat out more than she already is.

Remember; you can't do it all. By taking your cat to the veterinarian once per year, you'll ensure the optimal health of your friend. It's what a natural leader would do!

The Key Role Diet Plays in Feline Health

What you feed your kitty will directly influence her health. longevity, and quality of life. Cats fed poor-quality food can suffer from a myriad of problems, and normally live far shorter lives than their well-fed brethren. I cannot emphasis enough how vital it is to feed her the best food possible. Remember: good things in, good things out!

All things being equal, the perfect cat food is a mouse. Don't worry; I'm not going to suggest that you go out and purchase a case of rodents. But the statement does bear analysis.

Cats are true carnivores who do best on a high-protein diet, with that protein coming primarily from meat. Essential nutrients like taurine, niacin, arginine and vitamins A and D must be delivered to your cat in the form of a high-quality animal-based food. Your cat's protein needs are also somewhat specific; many of them cannot be synthesized from other foods, and must instead be consumed directly, from an appropriate meat source. Beans and rice won't cut it for kitty!

Cats also need a good amount of fat in their diet, also sourced from meat. Cats convert fat to energy, and also derive the essential vitamins A, D, E and K from animal fat. Hormone production, nerve function, skin and coat health, and many other bodily processes depend on fat. A particularly important fatty acid called archidonic acid, must be delivered to your cat through the consumption of animal fat.

Vitamins are as important for cats as for humans. They aid in energy production and the repair process, as well as certain blood-bone functions. And your cat's skin and coat depend on vitamins for optimal health. Again, only animal tissues can supply your cat with all her needed vitamins.

Minerals such as calcium, magnesium, phosphorus, sodium, iron, potassium, zinc and copper are all essential to your cat's health. Owners must be careful not to feed a food too high in minerals, however, as this can cause health issues, including kidney and heart disease. Most commercial foods provide more than enough minerals, with many actually providing too much, caused by excess bone meal. Raw food diets, though optimal in health, can actually contain inadequate mineral content, unless the owner formulates it properly. *(Note: I've included a good raw food diet in this chapter, with the proper ratios of nutrients.)*

Cats need some carbohydrates, but not nearly as much as we do. In fact, too many carbohydrates (found in abundance in commercial dry foods) can cause allergic reactions, gastrointestinal problems, flatulence, immune system breakdowns, pancreatic over-stimulation, and a host of other maladies. The fiber they provide does help somewhat with the digestive process, but, overall, carbohydrates are far less beneficial for cats than humans.

What Food Should You Feed?

The choices abound; the question is, what is the best diet for your cat? Besides the mouse diet, the best one is whichever provides your cat with optimal nutrition. Of course, affordability and scheduling also play a role; for instance, not everyone has the funds or time to feed a raw or home-prepared diet to their cats.

Let's take a look at your choices; I'll evaluate each, and then give you my recommendations:

Dry Food

Used by the majority of cat owners, dry kibble is perhaps the most con-venient of cat foods. With a long shelf life and relatively low per-unit cost, dry food makes economical sense for many.

Dry food quality can vary tremendously; some brands can be of very low quality, with high percentages of carbohydrates and fillers and poor-quality meat by-products instead of nutritious meat. Chemical preservatives, coloring agents, pesticide residues, mysterious "overseas" ingredients, and questionable vitamin/mineral contents make these foods a risky choice at best. Cats fed poor-quality dry foods all their lives often develop serious health problems later in life, particularly kidney disease and diabetes.

Higher-quality "premium" dry cat foods are available at some supermarkets and reputable pet stores. Though more expensive, they contain better ingredients, and are a step up from the bargain dry foods. Human-quality meat should be the first ingredient, with only natural preservatives such as Vitamin E used. The minimal grains used should be whole, cooked and organic, instead of grain "fractions"—grain husks, peanut shells, or even sawdust. The food should be nutritionally complete, and pass muster with your veterinarian. Choose foods with no artificial ingredients if you can. If you decide to feed a dry cat food, do your homework and find a company that manufactures its food at its own facility, instead of farming out the process to a third party.

My own opinion is somewhat tough on dry foods, even those made by reputable companies. More and more veterinarians are dissuading their clients from using dry food for their cats, for a number of reasons, including:

Compared to the optimal cat diet (there's that mouse again), kibble is quite high in carbohydrates. A wild cat's diet contains about five percent carbohydrates, while that of a domestic cat eating dry food equals about fifty percent. This imbalance causes the pancreas to over-produce insulin; over a period of years, the cat's insulin-producing cells can eventually shut down, resulting in diabetes, or chronically high blood sugar levels. Remember: the cat is an obligate carnivore whose diet should consist primarily of animal tissue!

Dry food has a low water content in comparison to canned food. As cats have a relatively low thirst drive, they need to get most of their water from the food they eat. Dry food does not provide this. Over time chronic dehydration can ensue, causing kidney problems.

Many dry foods provide protein derived from plant material, not animal. These proteins are harder for a cat to process.

Excess carbohydrates can over time irritate the cat's intestines, causing an onset of Irritable Bowel Disease (IBD). Too much grain, not enough meat!

Dry food can throw off the balance of minerals in a cat's diet, leading to the formation of stones in the urinary tract and bladder.

Cats fed dry food are at risk of obesity, due to the higher caloric value per unit than wet food.

Sorry to be so hard on dry food, but, as a natural cat owner, you need to know the truth when it comes to cat nutrition. Understand that plenty of cats eating dry food live long lives; if your cat is one of them, I congratulate you. But the simple fact is that a quality wet diet is superior to dry food over the long run.

Canned Food

Canned food, if formulated properly, can provide your pet with great nutrition. Like dry food, it has a long shelf life. Unlike dry, it more closely approximates the right ratios of protein, fat, carbohydrates and other nutrients. With moisture levels at fifty to seventy percent, it also better reflects a cat's need for water in her food.

Canned food is more expensive than dry food. And it isn't necessarily of better quality, especially if you buy economy brands at the supermarket. These use poor-quality meat sources, and often contain more carbohydrates than needed. Artificial coloring, chemical preservatives and other nefarious ingredients can cancel out benefits derived from feeding a wet product.

The moral is of course to buy the highest quality canned food you can. Shop at a reputable pet store, and check out the ingredient list before buying. Look for real meat (not by-products) as the primary ingredient, and a well-formulated recipe that provides all the needed vitamins, minerals, and ratios of protein, fat, and carbohydrates. Look for natural preservatives, and buy cans with the freshness date prominently stamped. As with dry food, stick with a company that formulates and manufactures its own food, instead of using a third party.

The "Pop-Top" Can Controversy

Reputable veterinary researchers have apparently discovered a link between hyperthyroid disease (or an overactive thyroid) and the use of "pop-top" cat food cans. Evidently the chemicals used to line these cans and allow the "pop-top" feature may be contributing to this problem. Though not yet definitive, the anecdotal evidence appears quite strong; because of this I'd recommend avoiding pop-top cans until more information on this controversy comes to light.

Semi-Moist Food

Packaged in single-serve plastic bags, these "mock ground meat" cat foods are popular with some cat owners. They keep well, and appear to be tasty to most cats. Don't be swayed by ease of use and palatability; these foods contain high amounts of artificial colorings and preservatives, binders, and unnecessary sugars. Though capable of providing your cat with adequate nutrition, these semi-moist foods are the least desirable of all offerings, in my humble opinion. The popularity of these "burger-like" meals appears due to their appeal to the human palate rather than the cat's; they look yummy, so we buy them. They are more expensive than canned or dry; I'd avoid them.

Homemade Cat Food

A growing number of cat owners prepare their cat's food at home, using fresh ingredients. Utilizing a variety of raw meats, a modicum of well-cooked vegetables and the appropriate vitamin/mineral supplements, this "raw" recipe best reflects a wild cat's natural diet. Short of rounding up those mice, this is the best you can do for your cat.

Let's talk about the raw food concept. Both cats and dogs have gastrointestinal tracts designed to digest raw meats better than our longer, less acidic system. Bacteria in most cases succumb to the feline's highly acidic stomach. Many people still avoid feeding raw food to their pets, viewing them as small people with the same dietary needs as a human child. "Be the cat" and don't make that mistake; cats are not people!

An optimal raw diet provides a cat with the best ratio of nutrients, and the highest percentage of beneficial amino and fatty acids, enzymes, vitamins, minerals and carbohydrates. And it also provides a cat with the right amount of water, built right into the food itself. This ensures your cat will be properly hydrated, avoiding kidney problems, stone formation, and other issues related to chronic dehydration. Plus, a raw diet is low in carbohydrates and has fewer calories per unit than dry kibble, helping the owner keep his or her cat's weight down.

Though a raw diet will cost more than a commercially prepared cat food, it won't be too much more expensive than a premium canned cat diet. Remember though that we are dealing not with a sixty-pound dog, but an eight- to twelve-pound cat. And if you prepare large amounts in advance and freeze it, you'll barely notice the additional cost.

Apart from the cost, there is also prep time, and the possible need for a meat grinder of some sort. A food processor will probably work provided you first take the time to chop large cuts of muscle meat up. Organ meats such as liver or kidney shouldn't pose a problem for a processor.

If you decide upon preparing your own fresh cat food, you must take care to buy the best cuts of meat available. That means premium human-grade meat, inspected and passed by the FDA. By doing so, you minimize any chances of the meat being inferior, or tainted with parasites. Always avoid feeding raw pork products to your cat, as they might contain the *trichina* worm, which causes trichinosis, a serious, life-threatening condition.

If you are concerned about bacterial or parasitic infection, feel free to blanch or microwave the meat first, for a minute or so. This will kill most infectious agents. For older cats or those with a history of immune or digestive issues, it might be advisable. Though cooking does destroy some essential amino acids and other nutrients, it will be minimal at best. The benefits of feeding the blanched or microwaved food will still far outweigh any commercial offerings.

If you decide on the raw diet, you cannot simply feed your cat raw meat. You must make sure that your cat gets all the necessary nutrients! In addition, I always recommend the addition of a daily cat vitamin/mineral supplement, to guarantee she's safely covered.

Be sure to switch your cat over gradually from a commercial food to the raw diet, to prevent diarrhea or other digestive issues. Take a month for the switch; gradually increase the amount of fresh food each day while reducing the amount of kibble or canned accordingly. Once she is eating fresh-only, realize that this diet will be less caloric than the commercial; you'll have to feed her more. And once your cat finishes eating, be sure not to store any leftovers from her dish; just toss it, to prevent disease and bacterial growth.

A Simple Home-cooked Recipe for Your Cat

Following is a basic recipe formulated to keep your cat healthy and happy for years. The proper serving size will vary according to the cat; try three heaping tablespoons per serving at first and adjust if necessary. The vitamin/mineral and taurine supplements should be added to one meal per day.

NATURAL DIET RECIPE

5 cups ground muscle meat (chicken, turkey, lamb, duck). Use several kinds if you like.

2 cups ground organ meat mix (kidney, liver, gizzards, heart). Be sure to include all in the mix.

2 well-ground chicken necks

1 cup well-cooked ground vegetables (boiled carrots or zucchini work well)

3 whole raw eggs

3 tablespoons bone meal

3 tablespoons olive or flaxseed oil

1 vitamin/mineral supplement per day (follow manufacturer's suggestions)

1 taurine supplement per day (follow manufacturer's suggestions)

If you desire, blanch or microwave the meat for one minute before grinding. Once mixture is blended, let cool, then store in the freezer in freezer-friendly containers. Defrost in the refrigerator and/or warm water when needed.

A Dietary Compromise

If the raw diet seems like too much work for you, try this compromise. Continue feeding your cat a premium commercial cat food, but slowly supplement it with some of the homemade mixture above. Reduce the commercial food by ten to twenty percent over a few weeks, replacing it with the raw mix. Feel free to increase the proportions of raw food if you desire; just do it slowly. By supplementing your cat's regular diet with the raw mix, you'll improve her health yet still maintain much of the convenience and affordability of her original diet. If the idea of raw food simply turns you off, choose a top-notch canned food (no pop-tops), then mix some of it into your cat's kibble, just as you would with the raw mix. Or simply switch over to a premium canned product over a few weeks time.

How the Home Set-up Affects Health

Your cat spends most of her time in and around the home, so it's your duty to make it a safe place. From top to bottom, you need to go over your home and ferret out potentially dangerous items or situations that a cat might get into. Realize that she is insatiably curious and highly mobile; areas which might seem safe to us could be lethal to your cat, so remember to "be the cat," and think in feline dimensions!

Toxins

Your home is filled with potentially toxic substances that can hurt your kitty. Just take a peek under your sink, in your garage, or in the utility room; you'll find a myriad of chemicals, solvents, cleaners, insecticides—you name it, it can cancel out all your cat's nine lives in a flash. A cat who gets into something such as anti-freeze, silver cleaner, acetone, or drain cleaner is pretty much finished; it's your job to prevent that. Even chocolate, raisins, or a common houseplant can be lethal!

Signs of poisoning can vary tremendously, from lethargy, irritable behavior or hyperactivity to respiratory distress, convulsions, drooling, diarrhea, excess urination or even paralysis and death. Poisons such as anti-freeze or liquid decongestants can actually taste good to a cat, making your vigilance even more vital. A list of toxic materials includes (but is not limited to) the following common household items:

- Any human pain reliever
- Alcoholic beverages
- Alcohol-based medicines, rubs and solvents
- All acid-based materials
- Detergents
- Bleach, ammonia, and other everyday household cleaners
- Insecticides
- Paint
- Motor oil, gasoline and any petroleum-based fuels
- All solvents, especially paint thinners and turpentine
- Lawn and garden fertilizers and weed killers
- Chocolate products and raisins

Garbage

With regard to any of these items, the safest course of action is to keep them all safely out of your cat's domain. That means behind *latched* cupboards, preferably up high, in a spot she cannot find a pathway to. With cupboards and other storage areas, also consider *back* entry; often a cupboard will be open in the back; if your cat finds a small hole in the drywall or even a small space between the cupboard and wall, she can access this lethal entryway.

Install baby-proof locks on all kitchen cupboards, especially below the sink and pantry. Clean all spills, and when possible, use organic products, such as manure instead of chemical fertilizer. And keep all prescription drugs in a safe, secure place, and not a medicine cabinet, which a cat can easily access.

Toxic Plants

Yes, plants can kill. Houseplants we consider harmless can sicken or kill cats if ingested in large enough quantities. Even garden plants can be toxic—another reason to keep kitty indoors.

The following is a list of common toxic indoor/outdoor plants. Though thorough, it is by no means complete; only your veterinarian can tell you for sure if a new plant is potentially harmful to your cat:

- Dieffenbachia
- Ivy
- Philodendron
- Poinsettia
- Mistletoe
- Marijuana
- Cactus
- Hydrangea
- Lily
- Bean foliage
- Azalea
- Hemlock
- Mushroom
- Yew
- Tomato leaves or any member of the nightshade family
- Tobacco
- Crocus and daffodil
- Oleander

If your cat goes outdoors, steer clear of any toxic garden plants, or place them in inaccessible spots (if that's possible). Unfortunately, you won't be able to stop your cat from visiting your neighbor's yard.

Indoors, provide your cat with some young wheat grass plants to satisfy her occasional craving for greens. Grow them yourself, or purchase at the pet store; then place the pot in a location separate from any other houseplants.

Power Cords and Electrical Outlets

Cats will chew on power cords, or stick a curious paw or tongue into an electrical outlet or exposed lamp socket. If yours does, it's basically lights out, so be sure your cat-proofing includes dealing with these. Hide any lamp or computer power cords beneath carpeting edges where they meet a wall (but never beneath areas of actual foot traffic) or behind moldings, and unplug anything you aren't currently using, such as a vacuum cleaner or hair dryer. Purchase plastic baby-guard outlet plugs for all your outlets, to prevent access. And be sure to keep bulbs in your lamps, unless you unplug them.

Doors and Windows

Leaving a door or window open to the outside often results in a cat escaping into the big outdoor unknown. If your cat is used to going in and out, she'll most likely come back (though not always). But if she is an indoor-only cat, she might become disorientated, and end up lost, injured, or adopted by another family. If you want fresh air, open a window but keep a sturdy screen closed. The same goes for a door; be sure to have a screen door securely locked before opening the main door. Be sure the windows in your children's rooms are secured also, and any back doors you might have. Teach your kids to properly close all windows and doors, too; I have personally had to search for a lost pet for this exact reason, so teach them well!

Have a proper identification tag on your cat in case she does disappear. A plastic or metal tag purchased at a local pet store will do; attach it to a collar that will not choke your cat if it gets caught on something. Proper cat collars are designed to either break away or stretch when caught.

You can also have your veterinarian implant a microchip ID into your cat, which can be scanned with the appropriate hand scanner at any veterinarian's office. It will hold all pertinent information needed to get her home to you. You can even get her tattooed with the proper info; many cat breeders do this with their prize cats.

First Aid

If in the unfortunate event your cat becomes injured, you'll need to be able to deal with it. Minor problems can usually be treated at home, while bigger problems may need first aid while you rush your cat to the emergency clinic.

First you'll need a proper cat first aid kit. It should contain:

- Rectal thermometer
- Gauze pads
- Adhesive tape
- Disinfectant solution
- Mineral oil
- A roll of gauze
- Tweezers
- Syrup of ipecac
- One emergency blanket
- A towel
- Swabs
- Rubbing alcohol

- Hydrogen peroxide

- Petroleum jelly

- Latex gloves

- Eyedropper

- Small scissors

- Veterinarian-approved hydrocortisone cream

Keep the emergency veterinarian clinic's telephone number handy, as well as copies of your cats vaccination records. Be sure to also have a cat carrier handy, to transport her to the clinic.

Taking Vital Signs

Knowing what your cat's vital signs are will help you determine her condition, and just what to do next. They include:

Temperature

Normal body temperature for a cat is between 100.5 and 102.5 degrees Fahrenheit. Anything outside those parameters can indicate illness or some sort of distress. Taking your cat's temperature can be traumatic for her; she's likely to try to bite or scratch. For this reason, unless it is essential, consider letting your veterinarian do it. This will help preserve your cat's trust in your handling of her.

If you absolutely need to take her temperature, first clean your rectal thermometer in warm soapy water then lubricate it with petroleum jelly. With a gloved friend holding her in a standing position, lift her tail and place a small amount of petroleum jelly on her anus. Then gently insert the thermometer straight into her anus about an inch or so. After a minute, remove it and note the temperature. If abnormal, call your vet.

Pulse Rate

Normal resting pulse for a cat should be about 120 beats per minute, though a variation of ten percent in either direction is acceptable. If outside this range, she could be ill. To take her pulse, place three fingers on the spot where a rear leg meets her body, where the femoral artery is located. It will take some practice, but eventually you will feel her pulse. Count how many you feel in ten seconds then multiply by six to get her pulse.

Respiration

A cat's normal resting respiration rate should be about twenty-five to thirty breaths per minute, though activity will increase it considerably. Determining her rate of respiration can be done while you are handling her; with a hand on her chest, feel her breathing, count how many in a ten second period, then multiply by six.

Emergency First Aid Techniques

Hopefully you will never need to perform emergency first aid on your cat. But if that day comes, as a natural cat owner you need to be ready. In any serious situation, your main goal should be to stabilize your cat's condition, so you can then transport her to an emergency veterinary facility as quickly as possible. Let's talk about the most common emergency situations first:

Vehicle Accidents

Cats and cars or trucks just don't mix; the cat who survives getting hit by one is a truly lucky soul. The best way to avoid this potential tragedy is, of course, to keep your cat indoors. If yours is an indoor/outdoor cat, though, you'll need to act quickly if she does get hit. First, stay cool and take stock of the situation. Is she conscious? Does she appear to have any broken bones? Is there bleeding? Remember that, even if there are no obvious injuries, you need to get her to the vet anyway, to check for internal damage.

If she appears seriously injured, you'll need to get her to the vet; but the issue of spinal injury comes into play. Any unnecessary movement can further damage her spine, so carefully place a towel, coat or blanket around her to restrict motion, taking great care not to move her. Then call the emergency clinic for further instructions.

If she has no apparent injuries, wrap her in a towel and transport her to the vet. Realize she may be in shock, and will possibly try to bite or scratch you. If garden gloves are handy, *use them*. You may even need to muzzle her with a sock, shoelace, or anything else available. Wrapping her in the towel should be sufficient in most cases; just be sure you do not obstruct her breathing. If possible, have a friend drive while you hold the cat still.

If you have no option but to transport a cat with possible spinal injury, find something flat and rigid such as a board, a garbage can lid or even a skateboard, and carefully move her onto it. Secure her, and then get to the clinic.

Shock

Shock happens when an injured cat's supply of oxygen falls too low. She'll have a low temperature and be disoriented. Her gums may be pale, and her pulse will be rapid or nearly undetectable. If you think your cat is in shock, wrap her in a towel or blanket and get to the vet as quickly as possible.

Blood Loss

If injury to your cat causes profuse bleeding, her blood pressure will fall, and she will drop into shock. If this is not addressed, she will die from lack of oxygen to the brain.

To deal with a bleeding wound, first immobilize the cat. Wear garden gloves if possible. Then apply direct pressure on the wound with a towel or gauze padding; keep pressure on for five minutes, then release and check for further bleeding. While doing this, have a vehicle ready to transport her to the vet. If bleeding continues, try compression bandaging; place a clean gauze pad on the wound, then wrap or tape it securely. While maintaining pressure, transport her to the vet.

Tourniquets should be avoided unless a major artery in a limb has been severed. You can use a shoelace, belt, tie, or strip of cloth to make a tourniquet; tie it around the affected limb above the wound, then insert a pencil or pen under the tourniquet and twist until tight enough to control the bleeding. Loosen it briefly every few minutes to keep blood in the limb, to prevent tissue death. In the meantime, have someone transport you to the emergency clinic.

Animal Assault

If your cat is injured by another animal, first be sure the attacking animal has been dealt with, and that you are not in danger yourself. Then access the wounds; if there is minimal bleeding, clean and dress, then get her to the vet. If bleeding is severe, deal with it per the directions above. During treatment, immobilize her with a towel, and wear gloves if possible.

Broken Bones

If your cat breaks a leg, immobilize it by carefully wrapping a hand towel around it, then taping it securely. Then wrap her in a coat or towel and transport her to the vet, being careful not to get bitten or scratched. If the break is a compound fracture with bleeding, you'll have to staunch the blood flow per the directions above.

Choking

If your cat chokes on an object, first see if you can remove it with your fingers or a pair of tweezers. Gloves are highly recommended! If you cannot see the object, perform the Heimlich maneuver. Put your cat on her side, then locate her last rib, closest to her abdomen. Place a hand just below this last rib, atop her diaphragm; then give two or three fast compressions with light force; if this does not work, increase the force of the compression to try to dislodge the object. During this procedure, you should be transporting her to the vet with a friend's help.

CPR

If your cat stops breathing but has a pulse, you will have to give her mouth-to-mouth. If her heart has stopped, you will have to combine mouth-to-mouth with chest compressions. Called *cardiopulmonary resuscitation* (CPR), it's a last-ditch effort that can save your cat's life. Keep in mind that this serious procedure should be performed while a friend transports you and your cat to the emergency clinic.

With your cat on her side, examine the inside of her mouth for foreign objects that might be obstructing her breathing. Look for breathing, and check her pulse. If she has a pulse but is not breathing, perform mouth-to mouth resuscitation by holding her mouth shut and placing your mouth over her nose, then giving two short, easy breaths. Remember she has tiny lungs, so go easy! If she does not begin breathing on her own, continue giving short easy breaths at the rate of fifteen per minute.

If she is not breathing and has no pulse, perform CPR. Place a thumb on her sternum, while bracing her back with your other hand. Apply compressions to the sternum with your thumb at about two per second; after giving ten compressions, give two mouth-to-mouth breaths. Then repeat. If a friend is available to help, have him or her give the compressions while you administer the breaths. CPR should be given on the way to the emergency clinic!

Bites or Stings

Though irritating, most insect bites are not life threatening to a cat, unless the cat has an allergic reaction to it. Luckily her coat will protect her from most stings, unless it happens to her face or pads. If your cat is stung, check for a stinger and remove it by brushing a credit card across the area. Then clean the area and get to the vet. If there is no stinger, still clean the affected area, then carefully observe her pulse and respiration. If she shows distress of any kind, see the vet.

Snakebites are serious business. If your cat gets bitten by a snake, clean the wounds, then consider using a tourniquet (if the bite is on a limb, the most common spot) as described earlier. Then get to the vet quickly! If the bite is on the face or an area where a tourniquet cannot be used, clean the wounds and get to the vet pronto.

Exercise!

Your cat needs regular activity to stay trim and healthy. Without it, she'll put on weight, lose muscle tone, and eventually run the risk of disorders such as diabetes. Additionally, a fat cat is a bored cat, and boredom leads to behavioral problems. As a natural owner, you'll need to get your cat moving a bit each day, to keep her healthy.

Unlike canines, cats in the wild do not pride themselves on lengthy aerobic activities; instead, they show bursts of predatory activity, interspersed with lots or rest. So, any exercise you encourage your cat to perform should reflect this. For example, chasing a toy or teaser around the room should be a series of quick, fast, excitable pursuits, and not a long drawn-out saga.

So, what activities can you get your cat to participate in? They can include:

Chasing Toys

Cats like chasing toys and teasers because of their predatory instincts. Any unpredictable movement will stimulate your cat to chase and pounce. If you encourage her to do so a few times each day, it will get her heart beating and her muscles moving. Mouse toys, ping-pong balls, teaser wands, wind-up or battery-operated toys—even balled-up newspaper can motivate her to chase and pounce. Try to keep her interested for five minutes, then quit. Two or three sessions per day will be more than enough to keep her fit, provided you do not overfeed her.

Stairs

Getting your cat to climb or descend stairs will get her heart pumping. To do so, entice her up a few steps with a toy or treat, then gradually increase distances by one step at a time. Or, try feeding her on the steps, moving her dish up a step each day until she is running all the way up for her dinner.

Fetch

Your cat will never rival a Labrador Retriever at fetching; nevertheless many cats will grab a tossed ball or mouse toy then return it for a repeat toss. If your cat likes to fetch, playing the game for a few minutes twice per day will really get her moving and happy. Ping-pong balls are particularly motivating to cats, especially on hard surfaces! Even if she doesn't return it to you, it's still great exercise.

Cat Company

One great way to keep a cat moving is to get two kittens instead of one, right from the start. If you have a kitten or young cat, consider getting another kitten for company. Avoid adopting an older cat, though, which might spawn a litany of territorial problems. And if you have an older established cat, only get a new kitten if you know she likes them. Determine that by testing her with a friend's kitten or young cat. Some shelters will now allow you to take a kitten home for a trial run, to see if she will get along with a resident cat.

Outdoors

Though I frown upon letting cats outdoors, doing so in a *supervised* manner might not be a bad way for your cat to get some exercise. Some cat owners construct an enclosed cat pen outside a door or window; with fenced-in sides and top, the cat can go outside without worry of getting lost or injured. Or, some owners actually teach their cats from kittenhood to wear a walking harness and go for short walks outside on leash. This *only* works if you start your cat out right from kitten-hood though; older cats will despise wearing a harness and being restricted by a leash. Only begin this with a kitten under the age of five months, and only if the kitten seems confident and eager. You start by purchasing a harness at the pet store then slowly desensitizing your cat to wearing it, over a period of a few weeks. Put it on her, give her a treat, then remove; gradually increase the time she wears it until she will tolerate it for a good half hour. Then clip a very light leash or string to it and let her drag it around the house. After a few days, pick up the end of the leash and follow her around; the idea is to let *her* determine the direction. Once she gets this, take her out in the yard and repeat; let her walk around, with you following, without tension on the leash. When ready to go inside, simply pick her up and go in. Be sure to give her treats and lots of praise during the whole procedure. And if she shows *any* stress at all over it, quit. Also, be sure never to take her out in busy areas, or near dogs!

Grooming

Though known for their legendary hygiene, cats nonetheless do need occasional grooming attention from owners. As a natural owner, you'll need to see that her coat, teeth, nails and overall appearance are main-tained in healthy fashion.

Regular brushing and combing will help stimulate the sebaceous glands in her skin, and encourage blood flow. Also, you'll remove excess hairs, which she might otherwise swallow during grooming; this will minimize hairballs. As an added bonus, scheduling regular grooming session from kittenhood on will help desensitize her to being handled, making needed handling much easier in the future.

Longhaired cats require more brushing and combing than short-haired cats. If your longhaired cat goes outdoors, she may be prone to matting of the hair, a potentially uncomfortable, tangled mass which cannot be combed out easily, and often needs to be cut out. By regularly brushing her, you'll avoid this. For a longhaired cat, you will need a good comb and brush; consult a groomer or pet store for advice on which will work best for your cat.

Begin by combing your cat for very short periods of time, making sure to praise and offer her treats. Gradually increase the time until she can tolerate a few minutes of it. Some cats actually like the feeling, while others merely tolerate it and wonder why you don't have them do the job themselves! After the combing, run a brush over her coat lightly, making sure to praise and reward. Most cats won't like too much brushing or combing around the face, rear and groin, so be sure not to linger in these areas.

If you encounter mats, try to gently tease them out with the comb. If a mat seems too dense to comb out, try removing it with scissors. But if the mat is too close to the skin, let a professional groomer take on the task. That way you won't risk hurting her, and she won't associate you with the discomfort.

If your cat is resistant to grooming, call on a pro to do the work. Again, it's not worth teaching your cat to fear handling from you. And you will avoid any potential scratches or bites.

Shorthaired cats are much easier. Usually they do not need combing; just a quick brushing every other day should do it. Use a comb around the tail, neck and face if need be, though.

When brushing a cat, spend a bit of time going "against the grain"; this will help expose her skin, so you can check for parasites, sores, or any other type of skin abnormality.

Nails

Despite your cat's use of her scratching posts, you may need to trim her nails every month or so. Not doing so may lead to her nails getting caught in carpets, furniture, drapes or clothing.

Try to cut your cat's nails only if she appears confident and open to handling. If she is timid and resistant, don't risk it; instead use a professional groomer, who is used to cats less than enthusiastic about the procedure.

Early on in your cat's life, begin handling her paws for a brief period of time during the day, while praising and rewarding with treats. During the session, lightly press on her toes to extend her nails, then let go. Try this twice each day for a week or so. Eventually extend her nails out long enough for you to get a good look at them. If her nails are white, you'll see the "quick," or the vein inside the nail that stops short of the tip. The objective is to *never* cut the quick, as this will be painful. Only clip the very tips of the nails, avoiding the quick. If your cat has opaque nails, you won't see the quick; you will need to be very careful and only cut the very tip each time. If in doubt, err on the side of caution and cut less.

While extending her nails, begin briefly touching them with your clipper, purchased at a quality pet store. Praise and reward! Do this for several days before moving on.

Now, extend a nail, touch it once or twice, then confidently snip a *tiny* bit of the tip off. Praise and reward, then try another. If you only cut one or two at this point, it's fine. Your objective should be to eventually get one paw done during a session. After four sessions she will have a perfect manicure!

Remember: nail trimming takes confidence and a deft touch. If you have any reservations, defer to a professional groomer!

A Word on Declawing

Many cat owners opt to have their cats declawed in order to prevent damage to furniture, persons, or other pets. The procedure is not simply a glorified manicure, but a surgical procedure in which the claws are detached from the cat's toe bones. Most often performed on the front claws, declawing is in actuality an amputation of part of the cat's anatomy, in order to manage a behavior which could be easily modified without such drastic measures.

Those who opt for declawing often either have expensive furnishings they wish to protect or a cat with a history of some type of play or defensive aggression. In either case, the motive is largely selfish at best.

Those cat owners who value their furnishings above the safety and well-being of a cat are not natural cat owners, having no real understanding of feline behavior. The vast majority of cats will prefer using scratching posts over sofas or drapery. If provided with at least two thirty-inch-high sisal scratching posts, placed in the living room and where the cat sleeps, she should leave the furnishings be. By taking preventive measures, such as double-sided sticky tape, aluminum foil, and sprays of water from a plant sprayer bottle, most owners should be able to direct scratching to the appropriate post.

In addition to traumatizing the cat physically and emotionally, declawing removes her ability to climb effectively or to defend herself. This can be fatal for a cat attempting to escape from a dog, coyote, or raccoon. Why condemn her to such a fate?

For those owners who cannot get their cats to stop scratching inappropriately, veterinarians are able to apply plastic claw caps to the front claws, effectively rendering them harmless. The caps, however, must be replaced about every month due to claw growth and glue degradation. Also, cats with claw caps lose much of their ability to climb or defend.

I would never declaw a cat. I consider it not only cruel, but an admission of defeat on the part of an owner. I am a natural cat owner; are you?

Bathing

Everyone knows that cats hate water (except tigers of course), and will move heaven and earth to avoid getting a bath. But sometimes it can't be avoided; she might get into a messy substance, or become covered with mud or waste. She might even get a potentially toxic substance on her that has to come off; whatever the reason, you need to be prepared to bathe her if necessary.

Bathing a cat is another grooming activity that is best started young. Nothing is harder than bathing a timid adult cat who has never suffered through one before. If your cat gets filthy and doesn't appear willing to let you clean her, look up a groomer who will play the heavy and save you from the grief.

First, you'll want to bathe her in the kitchen sink. Purchasing a rubber hose attachment will greatly help too, allowing you to properly direct the water instead of maneuvering the cat around. Placing a rubber mat down will also help her with traction, making her feel a bit safer. But before this, start by putting her in the sink and giving her a treat or two. Do this a few times each day for a week. Then, with a pan of warm water beside you, put her in the sink, massage her a bit, then wet a sponge in the water and gently rub it on her until her coat gets damp. Towel her off, praise and reward. Repeat this for a few days.

Now for the main event. With the spray attachment and hose ready, adjust the water until comfortably warm, then wet the cat down from neck to tail, avoiding the head. Massage the water in then towel her off and reward. If she tolerates this, you have accomplished a lot!

The final step is to add a veterinarian-approved shampoo to the procedure. After wetting her down again, quickly massage the shampoo in, then rinse thoroughly and towel off. Avoid using a hair dryer in an attempt to dry her, if you want to survive through the day.

I must reiterate: if you have *any* reservations about bathing her, or if she isn't cooperative, seek out a qualified groomer to take on the task. It's just not worth the stress!

Ears

Regularly checking your cat's ears is a vital part of keeping her healthy and happy. Parasites, dirt, fungi, infections, wax buildup—any number of disorders can make her life miserable. Cats with ear problems might shake their heads incessantly, scratch at them, or even walk with their heads canted to one side. If you see this, it could be an ear infection, requiring veterinary help.

To prevent ear problems, inspect her ears regularly, and be prepared to clean them. To do so, first get your cat used to being in your lap.

Stroke and massage her. Once she tolerates this, quickly look into each ear, checking for anything unusual. If you can, also sniff each ear for any abnormal smell, which could indicate infection. If you find anything unusual, see your veterinarian. But if you see dirt or wax, you can dip a cotton swab into mineral oil and gently swab the dirt away, being very careful not to go far into the ear canal. If the dirt is too far down or you are not confident, let the veterinarian or groomer take care of it. And do not force a timid cat to tolerate this, it's better to let a professional deal with it.

Teeth

Your cat's teeth are important to her, so it pays to inspect them once per week. Tooth decay, abscesses, chipped teeth or gum disease can become a serious health issue, so it's definitely worth a peek.

Only try this if your cat is confident and welcoming to inspection! A timid cat may bite, so, if in doubt, see your veterinarian.

With your cat in your lap, gently massage and pet her until she purrs. Then confidently place a hand atop her head, with thumb and forefinger at the corners of her mouth. Hook them in so the tips of your fingers are in under her lips, near the molars. Then tilt her head back quickly until her nose points up; this should open her mouth up enough for you to see her teeth and gums. Quickly look for anything abnormal: chips, infections, food debris, bleeding—anything needing attention. Then let go and praise her mightily!

A Word on Neutering

Responsible owners should have their cats neutered, to prevent a surplus of cats, and to minimize unwanted behaviors such as aggression, marking and roaming. But exactly when should it be done? Recently the timing of neutering (spay for the female, castration for the male) has become a subject of debate. Most shelters today neuter kittens as young as eight weeks of age, as a means of preventing unwanted births later on. Though supporters of this practice mean well, a growing number of research veterinarians now believe that early neutering can negatively affect both physiological and cognitive development in cats.

Reproductive hormones do more than just control the development of the reproductive system; in fact they regulate the development of many non-reproductive systems, including the brain, musculoskeletal system, central nervous system, vascular system, and others. Without the moderating effects of sex hormones, these systems can develop improperly.

My main concern is the effects of premature neuter on cognitive development. Research done at several leading veterinary colleges shows that brain development appears to rely somewhat on the presence of reproductive hormones; remove them prematurely and the cat's future "IQ" may suffer.

Unlike dogs, cats are often allowed to wander indiscriminately. Plus, cats come into estrus (or heat) much more often than dogs; when these two factors are combined, a population explosion occurs. Millions of unwanted kittens and cats are therefore euthanized each year.

Some compromise must be reached. Though cats should have the right to develop to their highest physical and mental potentials, they must also be protected from overpopulation resulting in mass euthanasia. My own recommendation to clients is to have female cats neutered at six months of age, before the onset of their first estrus, and in the case of males, any time between six and eight months. This will allow for ample cognitive and physiological development, yet still prevent unwanted pregnancies. If owners also keep their cats indoors, the odds of unwanted pregnancies wither to nothing.

If your cat was neutered as a kitten, don't worry. The effects of early neuter will hardly be noticed if you follow the secrets, and do what you can to enrich and teach.

Most shelters will not allow you to adopt a kitten until it has been neutered. Some, though, will allow you to "pre-pay" for a neuter, requiring you to get it done by the time a cat is five or six months old.

If you can find a shelter willing to agree to this, go for it. This "pre-pay" contract is more often offered to people wishing to adopt female kittens, as the spay procedure can be tougher on ten-week-old kittens than can castration.

Another compromise for ensuring both cognitive development and population control would be for veterinarians to perform tubal liga-tions or vasectomies on young cats, followed up at six or eight months by neutering. This would allow for the beneficial regulatory effects of reproductive hormones on non-reproductive systems, while still ensuring that no unwanted kittens are born. Unfortunately, these proce-dures are expensive, and rarely practiced. Perhaps, in light of current research, veterinarians might begin to consider this option.

Respect the Status Quo

Most cats do not like change, unless delivered in negligible doses. Owners who subject their cats to unpredictable shifting home conditions therefore run the risk of generating a litany of undesirable cat behaviors, from litter box mishaps to destruction or even aggression. Maintaining an established, comfortable routine in your cat's life then becomes one of the most essential things the natural owner can do to ensure harmony in the home. To truly "be the cat," you'll need to understand this fundamental cat fact.

Why Cats Loathe Change

Let's face it: cats are not as adaptable to the environment as dogs or people. They like things stable because it creates a territorial comfort zone for them. They are somewhat obsessive-compulsive in this respect; if you rearrange the furniture, paint the kitchen or (heaven forbid) go on vacation for two weeks, your cat may disappear into the fabric of your home and not speak to you for weeks. And if you bring a new pet into the home—well let's not even go there right now. Suffice it to say your cat likes the tidy, the unchanging, the obvious, because it presents less to worry about and adapt to. If a feline predator knows her territory well, she'll tend to be content; if her territory and everything in it constantly changes, it creates stress and doubt. It's as simple as that. Remember: your cat is a predator whose territory is your home. Constantly redefining that territory creates an insecurity that will in

turn cause her to act out in some way. It would be the same for a
bobcat who suddenly finds that three new bobcats have moved into
the neighborhood, followed by a new golf course and hiking trail.
That bobcat would flip, and probably relocate.

Consistency Is the Key

As a natural cat owner, your job is to create a congenial atmosphere for
your cat, one which best guarantees she'll be calm and confident. When
she goes on patrol of your home, she sniffs, scratches, touches, and
notices; she likes things in their proper place. If she senses something
new she will automatically go into an analytical mode which, though
not necessarily bad, might cause her to do something that doesn't fit in
with your idea of domestic pet ownership. For instance, if you let a
friend's dog into the home for a few minutes, your cat will probably
disappear under a bed until the crude beast leaves. Then she may come
out, sniff out the course of the invader, and mark or scratch over it as a
way of reclaiming territory. Some cats will even do this if new people
visit; a good number will at the very least disappear until the interlopers are gone.

One of the prices of domesticity is that the cat must fit into the territorial parameters you set for her. You can make that as easy as possible
by avoiding wild fluctuations in the environment.

One of the biggest causes of lost cats is due to relocation to a new
neighborhood. New home, new neighborhood, new furniture—a feline
nightmare. The cat, ripped from its familiar territory and tossed into a
new one (one ruled by other phantom cats) feels at risk. If allowed outdoors, she is quite likely to wander off in search of her old digs. The
result is a lost cat, one who often ends up in a shelter.

What can you do to maintain your cat's territorial sanity? The best
solution is to try your best to keep things as stable and familiar as possible. This refers not only to the physical surroundings and the arrangement of furniture etc., but to temporal routines as well. If your cat is
used to a certain schedule, any major changes to it will stress her out.

Owners who change shifts at work, for instance, often get the cold shoulder from their cats for a while, or at the very least find their cats to be somewhat lost and worried. Such changes sometimes lead to litter box mishaps, destructive behavior, excess vocalizations, or even redirected aggression.

No one is saying that you need to structure your entire life around your cat's mental well-being. But you can work on maintaining a certain status quo in the home. For instance, having impromptu parties at random hours will stress your cat out, as will playing loud music, or letting other pets into the home. The same goes for timing: if you tend to do things at the same general times during the day, try to stick to that schedule. If you feed her at 7:00 p.m., don't suddenly start feeding her at 4:30 p.m. If you have an evening routine during which you sit on the sofa and watch television while she sits on your lap getting petted and talked to, don't suddenly abandon that tradition. She likes it, and looks forward to it.

How to Introduce Change

Obviously change will occur. People come and go; homes are bought and sold; furniture is replaced; rooms are painted or expanded. You have a baby or two, marry or divorce, or acquire new pets. Though it is ultimately your decision, there are ways to introduce change to your cat without precipitating too much stress for her.

The key is to go slow and not to be demonstrative with change. For instance, do you really need to replace every stick of furniture at once? It's a much better idea to do so one piece at a time, and to place the new piece in the position of the old piece, at least in the beginning. Or, if removing the carpeting in favor of hardwood floors, bridge the change by putting down a number of area rugs throughout the home. If you must replace her food dish, leave the old one down beside the new one for a week; place most of the food into the new dish while dropping a bit in the old one, eventually switching over completely to the new dish.

Painting? Do so one room at a time, starting with those rooms your cat rarely goes into. The same goes for spring cleaning; do so one room at a time instead of in one fell swoop. And be sure to limit your use of cleaners during the cleaning process, to prevent the chance of a toxic reaction, and to minimize the olfactory impact.

Changing a scratching post or kitty condo? Do so in the same manner you would the food dish. Place the new one near the old one and let her get used to it. Only after you see her regularly using the new one should you remove the old one.

Switching your cat over from an indoor/outdoor lifestyle to indoors only? Try doing it gradually, over a month or so, instead of cold turkey. Cutting down on her outdoor time by ten minutes per day will make the transition much easier, particularly if you adopt the enrichment techniques described earlier in the book. It will still be traumatic for her, but the graduated attempt will lessen adverse reactions. Just think moderation and subtlety, rather than sudden and extreme.

The same goes for emotions. Your cat will much prefer a levelheaded, calm, reliable owner to one whose emotions and habits are all over the map. Angry one minute, loving the next—that won't cut it with your cat. You'll confuse her and create disharmony. Remember: you are most likely a maternal figure to her. Who wants a nutty, unpredictable "mommy dearest" around? Being composed, dependable and trust-worthy, instead of flighty, vulnerable and capricious will go a long way in keeping your cat happy and problem-free.

New People or Pets

Rare is the cat who takes to a new person or pet without some emo-tional drama. Sure, there are confident, doggish cats who take it all in stride; many do not though, needing a break-in period to accommodate the new social dynamic. It's just the nature of the cat talking.

Unlike a dog, it is not essential to have your cat accept other people or pets; it just makes life a bit easier, and helps her gain a more relaxed perspective on life. More social interaction can also help enrich your cat's life, provided it is not forced upon her. Too much social input, especially for a timid cat, can actually cause more harm than good, so use your best judgment, and never force your cat to socialize.

The best way to get new people into her life is to start her out early, in kittenhood if possible. Have family and friends interact with her every day, especially in a playful, supportive way, using toys, teasers and treats to endear themselves to her. Having two kittens will also help open both up to additional socialization, not only from people, but from other pets as well. Kittens will even get along wonderfully with sweet dogs if raised with them from the get-go.

For older cats, consider having a trusted friend or two come over for regular visits, during which time they sit passively on the sofa reading, talking to you, or watching television. Give him or her a few cat treats to hold; if your cat comes by to investigate, have your friend drop one or two treats onto the floor. Consistently doing this will condition your cat to think that the new person means good things. You can also have friends or family feed your cat; even if she does not come up to the person, his or her smell will be on the food. A subtle desensitization will take place as the cat begins to associate the scent with the meal.

If your older cat is a bit more outgoing, encourage other people to play with her, or even brush or massage her briefly. If she will accept this from someone outside the home, you've accomplished a lot!

Be very particular about allowing children to interact with your cat. Only considerate kids should be allowed to associate with her. Little ones have a habit of pulling on ears and tails, teaching the cat to fear small humans. Teach your own children to be respectful and patient. Read portions of this book to them, and get them to feed, groom and play with your feline in a calm and civil manner.

Bringing new pets into the home of an established cat can be challenging; if your cat is happy with the status quo, consider letting things be. But if for some reason you must bring in a new pet, refer to The Social Life of Cats in Secret Three, and Social Enrichment around the Home in Secret Five.

New Food

You cannot change your cat's diet overnight without expecting problems. First, even if she likes the new food right off, your cat will most likely have adverse gastrointestinal reactions if switched over quickly. Cats cannot easily adapt to a new food; they must instead be weaned off of one and onto the other over a period of a few weeks. Doing so will help prevent diarrhea and vomiting, and will also increase the chances that she will accept the new food's flavor, texture, smell and presentation. They are fickle, you know; by reducing the old food by five or ten percent each day and replacing it with an equal amount of new food, you will minimize the chances of rejection and digestive upset.

The Sanctity of the Litter Box

Think about how important a comfortable, quiet, private commode experience is to you. Would you appreciate having your bathroom suddenly moved to a noisier location? Or having the toilet seat changed over to a less comfortable design? Or being forced to use a less desirable, smellier brand of toilet tissue? I think not!

The same rules apply to your cat and her experience with her litter box. Once used to it, she won't appreciate its being moved. And, she won't take kindly to a new design, or even a change in the type of litter used. Too many owners monkey around with the litter box set-up, only to find that they have actually caused problems that didn't exist before. If your cat likes the current set-up, why change? Why buy that super-duper, multi-leveled, self-cleaning, covered pet store monstrosity when the simple litter box you have now works perfectly? More so than nearly any other area, your cat wants her litter box to stay the same. If she likes it and is using it properly, keep it! Stick to the same litter also, as changing brands is one of the surest ways to disrupt her housetraining habits.

One of the few reasons to alter the litter box situation in your home is if you are acquiring a new cat. You should have at least one litter box per cat, to prevent territorial stress. When adding a new box, your old cat may begin using it, or decide to stick to the old one, while the new cat or kitten uses whichever box happens to be available at the time. Your established cat may lay claim to one or the other though; that's okay, as there will always be one free. It's like putting in a new bathroom to ease the tensions between teenagers!

The other cause for change would be a possible allergic reaction to the type of litter used. If you and your veterinarian determine this to be the case, you'll have no choice but to switch out the litter. Most allergic reactions cats have to litter are to the highly scented types; good old clay-based litter usually works fine with the more sensitive felines. You'll need to switch out the litter quickly, to avoid the allergic reaction; just be prepared for some temporary housetraining problems. Some cats won't care, while others will pout and use the ficus tree or your dirty laundry as alternative toileting areas. What can I say; they are fickle.

Moving

Relocating to a new home in a new neighborhood is tough for a cat. Used to the status quo, just about everything changes. Her territory, once well established, is pulled out from under her. Smells, dimensions, sounds—nearly everything is foreign. The layout of the new home is different; even the furniture often changes. Add to that the scent of new paint, and of the former owners (and their pets) and you have one confused kitty.

Owners who let their cats outside sometimes lose their pets when moving to new digs. Once let out into the new neighborhood, a relocated cat finds herself deep in the territory of other cats; she can smell them, and knows that she will soon be confronted and challenged as an interloper. This is not a fun feeling. Ever move to a new town when you were young? Remember the looks you got when walking into the new school? Multiply that times a hundred and maybe you'll understand your cat's situation. She'll have to carve out her own small territory, and most likely fight off a few feline thugs along the way. And she may decide to simply take off in search of her old digs, resulting in a lost cat.

The solution is not as simple as simply keeping your cat indoors. Yes, that *is* the solution, especially if moving into a more densely populated, urban area; but if your cat has been used to outdoor access her whole life, suddenly restricting her may cause behavioral problems. Sometimes it's just excess vocalizations, pacing, or pawing at windows and doors for a few weeks. But other times it becomes a major problem, with house-training setbacks, redirected aggression, destructive behavior—the whole gamut. See what you did? Seriously—letting your cat outside creates so many problems for the majority of owners that I just don't see the advantage. If you do move, consider trying to keep your world-traveling cat indoors. If she acts out terribly, you might be able to set up an enclosed cat pen in the yard or balcony, as discussed in the Outdoors section of Secret Six. Giving her regular access to this type of controlled situation could serve as a good compromise in her mind.

For an indoor-only cat, moving is less traumatic. But she will still be confused and a bit stressed. To minimize this, consider restricting her to one or two rooms at first. Move her litter box in there with her, and her food and water dishes. After a day or two, she'll begin to acclimate to the new smells and sounds; then, slowly expand her access to the new home, while making sure to keep windows and doors closed. Put out her toys, and encourage her to play with them and you. If she likes to fetch ping-pong balls or stuffed mice, by all means play with her in the new living room. Welcome any amount of attention from her; otherwise be observant and supportive.

Tiptoe Change into Her Life

The bottom line with changing your cat's environment: do it quietly, slowly, sneakily, with no demonstrative actions or slapdash dramatics. And always make it seem beneficial to her by creating accompanying perks she knows and loves. If you do, unexpected behavioral problems will be kept to a minimum. And always review a change you make beforehand; is it truly necessary? If it ain't broke, don't change it, cats always say. To truly *"be the cat,"* you must think this way. Really—*why change?*

The Natural Owner's Quick Guide to

Solving the Most Common Cat Problems

Cat owners who adopt the Seven Secrets will happily experience far fewer problem behaviors with their pets. Nevertheless, behavioral setbacks will pop up from time to time. For that reason, Part Three provides cat owners with quick solutions to the most common behavioral problems they might face with their felines. If you have issues not covered here or in the rest of the book, consult the library, the Internet, your veterinarian or a pet behaviorist.

Antisocial Behavior

Though less social than dogs, cats who shy away from contact with people are showing antisocial tendencies. Taken to the extreme, antisocial behavior can result in aggression, though this is rare. A scared cat who shies away is antisocial, while one who attacks in a defensive or offensive manner has taken her tendencies one step farther into aggression.

Many cats are by nature shy, and that's okay. But yours should be willing to spend time with you, and with other members of the household. If she won't, something's amiss. She should not be expected to buddy up to strangers though; that's just not required of a cat.

When a newly adopted cat shows antisocial tendencies, give her some time to acclimate. Most cats will come around in time and learn to have faith in their owners, provided those owners remain patient, calm and placid. Remember to let your cat set the tone of the relationship! Offer treats, speak softly, and let her come to you. Also, consider putting her on a regular feeding schedule instead of free-feeding, as this will connect you with her food, always a good social motivator.

Eventually she will get curious enough to pop up into your lap. When she does, pet her, but let her decide when the session is over. If each session remains a pleasant experience, she'll come back for more.

If she shows anti-social tendencies towards others, all you can do is have trusted friends and family come over regularly and be available if and when she decides to show. When people do come over, have them remain somewhat stationary, on a sofa for instance. If the cat starts investigating, the person can toss a treat or two down, to begin the association between strangers and food. Eventually she will learn to tolerate the interlopers!

Realize that a shy cat will in most cases remain shy throughout her life. You can moderate it though, through the techniques I have mentioned. Just accept the way she is while still quietly working on socialization.

Biting or Scratching

Not necessarily considered outright aggression, a cat who bites or scratches can be a confusing experience for an owner, who wonders why he or she is being treated in such an antisocial manner. Often a cat will be sitting in your lap getting petted; suddenly she deems she has had enough attention, reaches back, and bites or scratches. Not hard enough to necessarily break skin; just enough to warn you off. After, she may act as if nothing ever happened.

Most cats have a built-in tolerance limit for physical attention. Once reached, yours will signal you that enough is enough. Some cats just get up and leave, while others bite or scratch. More common with unneutered cats and those who spend time outdoors, this behavior is a proven way for your cat to get the message across.

Too much physical attention is foreign to cats. That's why it is important for you to let your cat set the tone of your relationship. Develop a sense of when your cat is about saturated with your attentions, then stop before she reacts. That's a big part of *being the cat*. Also, handling a cat too roughly, or in an area she might deem off-limits (such as the rump, groin, or neck) can invoke a quick warning scratch or bite.

Some cats are less tolerant than others, and have a shorter fuse, but any cat will react this way if she feels put upon. Realize that it isn't an abnormal behavior, per se, it's just that we define it as such. Using effective feline empathy, you'll understand that your cat is just communicating in catlike fashion her discomfort with the excessive handling.

Owners who roughhouse with their cats or kittens encourage the biting/scratching behavior, as they assume the behavior is simply part of the physical process. If kittens in a litter were accustomed to playing hard with each other, those cats will be more likely to use the behavior later on in life, on their owners.

A sick or an injured cat might bite or scratch when a sore area is touched. If you suspect she has any pain or discomfort, get her to the veterinarian for a diagnosis.

To prevent biting or scratching from becoming an issue:

- **Get your cat neutered before she reaches sexual maturity.**

- **Be sure she has no injuries or illnesses that could be causing the protective biting or scratching behavior.**

- **Limit petting sessions to short periods of time, and always allow her to determine when they start, and when they finish.**

- **Socialize your cat from kittenhood in a gentle, non-threatening manner. Include regular grooming sessions and massage.**

- **Keep your cat indoors, to prevent her from developing a suspicious, protective mindset.**

- **Let her set the tone of your relationship.**

Aggression

True aggression in a cat is a sobering thing. Given their superior speed and athletic abilities, cats are quite capable of hurting you; therefore you'll want to avoid cat aggression whenever possible.

There are many different forms of cat aggression, so let's look at them each:

Fear aggression occurs when a cat fears for her safety and lashes out in defense. A normal response to a perceived danger, you can normally avoid the occurrence of this type of aggression by keeping your cat safe and protected from threats. Outdoor cats will, as a matter of course, show fear aggression when confronted by cats, dogs, other animals, or people or vehicles that may mean them harm. A shy cat in the home could also display fear aggression if someone or something frightens her. Cats taken from their littermates too early (before seven weeks old) can often show fear aggression, as they did not get a chance to learn proper social etiquette while young.

To avoid fear aggression, keep your cat indoors, and socialize from kittenhood on. Also, know your cat's temperament and social limitations, and avoid putting her into situations she cannot tolerate. Let your cat determine the tone of the relationship! Don't even consider adopting a cat before her seventh week; but if you do, be sure to get her together with other kittens immediately so she can properly develop her cat social skills.

Dominance (or territorial) aggression occurs when a cat uses her innate sense of status, privilege or territorial tenure to control or repel others who she deems threatening to those factors. To prevent this type of aggression, have your cat neutered before she reaches sexual maturity.

Keep her indoors to limit her territorial aspirations, and to prevent cat-to-cat conflicts. Prevent unpredictable challenges to her territorial nature in the home by keeping strange pets away, and by coaching visitors not to force their attentions on the cat. Keep her home territory stable and free from upsetting "invasions." Socialize her with persons and pets she tolerates, and allow her to decide when she will be handled or played with.

Food aggression and possessive aggression are closely related, in that your cat considers her food, toys, and other belongings to be her own personal property. It is normal for her to protect her things from another pet, but not from you, as you are the "mother cat." Stray cats are famous for showing food or possession aggression, as they have had to fight for every morsel or item.

For food aggression issues between pets, be sure to feed them separately, in separate rooms. Be sure to have separate food and water dishes. If the aggression is occurring between a dog and a cat, feed the cat in a separate room, or on an elevated counter which the dog cannot reach. If the food aggression is directed at a person, go to a free-feeding schedule, to lessen the cat's food drive. Then begin to associate yourself with the actual delivery of food; let your cat see you placing food in her dish. Give her treats during the day to further the association between you and food.

For possessive aggression, try overloading her with toys, to diffuse her possessive drive. Also, use toys that require you to participate, such as feather teasers. Avoid playing fetch, as she might not surrender the toy without a fight.

Prey aggression, closely related to food or possessive aggression, is a normal instinct for all cats. They are hunters, after all. If presented with the chance to kill a bird, odds are your cat will. If she begins stalking you, though, that's a different matter. If this occurs, get her some fun toys that she can hunt down, such as a feather teaser, a battery-operated or wind-up toy, or even a ping-pong ball. Being sure to stimulate her prey instincts each day with a good play session should alleviate her desire to jump you!

Hereditary aggression, caused by poor breeding, cannot be effectively modified by you, as it is caused by faulty genetics. If you suspect that your cat has profound aggressive tendencies, have her evaluated by your veterinarian, who may be able to prescribe medications to moderate the behavior.

Sexual aggression occurs during the courtship ritual. Anyone who has heard cats mating knows that it isn't exactly a loving interaction! To avoid this, simply get your cat neutered, and keep her fuzzy butt indoors!

Maternal aggression occurs when a nursing female shows aggressive intent toward anyone who happens to come too close to her kittens. It's a normal reaction, but one which can vary tremendously from cat to cat. Some will let their owners handle the kittens without issue, while others will turn into little buzz saws; it's a function of instinct, tempered somewhat by personality.

Hopefully you are not allowing breeding to go on. It's really the job of the professional and not the owner. The "miracle of birth" can be seen on the Discovery Channel; no need to create more cats in need of homes.

If your cat does have kittens, be sure to give her a warm, quiet place to nest and care for them. Let her do her job, and try not to handle the kittens for at least a few days, unless necessary. Eventually, when the mom goes off to eat or use the litter box, handle the kittens gently one at a time. When she comes back she will smell you on them. This shouldn't cause problems, and will in fact help her associate the kittens with you, allowing future handlings to be less conflicted in her mind. But, unless she appears open to it, avoid handling the kittens in her presence.

After she has weaned the kittens, get her spayed. She doesn't need to have another litter!

Paternal aggression occurs when a male cat (or tom) tries to kill a litter of kittens he did not sire in an attempt to stop a competitor's bloodline from succeeding, and to bring a female quickly back into heat. Barbaric, yes, but very much a normal cat instinct, particularly in the wild. You won't need to deal with this unless you have a nesting female and a male in the same household, one who did not sire the litter. If you do, you are a silly goose. No, seriously—keep males away until the kittens are at least eight weeks old, and get him neutered!

Redirected aggression happens when a cat, stressed out by a certain situation, redirects her frustrations at another, usually innocent victim. This happens with humans too; anyone who has ever gotten into an argument and then lost his or her temper with someone else knows what I mean. It's a somewhat "normal" reaction to untenable stress. All you need do to prevent it in your cat is to keep stress levels as low as possible. Keep the number of cats low; avoid excess handling if possible; keep your cat indoors; just let her be, right after a traumatic event, instead of coddling her; and make the home environment as safe as possible.

Litter Box Problems

One of the biggest causes of cats being returned to shelters, inappropriate cat elimination can be a terrible experience for all. But a litter box-trained cat doesn't simply stop using her box for no reason; instead, something is usually wrong.

The first thing to check if your cat begins eliminating outside her box is her overall health. If she is sick or injured, she might evidence this by inappropriate elimination. Kidney or bladder problems, urinary tract infections, stones, intestinal disorders—almost anything can set it off. Even a wound from a fight or a sprain or abscess can throw her off. If she is having housetraining accidents in random places and not choosing the same spot each time, she may be ill or injured. Get her to the veterinarian for a checkup, to rule it out.

Next, check the litter box itself. Did you change brands of litter? If so go back to the old brand. Are you cleaning it often enough? A dirty box will cause a cat to seek out another spot to eliminate, so keep things tidy! Having too few boxes can also cause the problem. Have at least one litter box per cat!

Emotional trauma can also trigger litter box problems. A move, a new pet, spouse or child, a fight, or even a change of furniture can incite a temporary loss of good habit. Abuse, a difficult grooming session—nearly anything can create enough stress to trigger accidents. To prevent this, try to follow Secret Seven's advice: *Respect the status quo!* Consistency is the key to good housetraining habits. Make changes slowly, and avoid replacing the litter box if possible. Don't overwhelm her with too much change too quickly; instead, do it gradually.

If you suspect emotional trauma, try to identify what happened or what changed. Return things to the way they were if possible, and prevent the traumatic event from happening again. She will likely return to her good habits once stress levels subside.

Marking behavior happens when a cat decides there is a challenge to her territorial dominion. If for instance your male cat suddenly sees a strange cat loitering outside the window, he may spray the window in objection, to exercise his dominance and territorial claim. Though marking can be denoted by scratches, it is usually a spray of urine onto an appropriate spot that marks the perimeter of the cat's territory. Multiple cats can mark out territories within a home, especially if a new cat is introduced.

Unneutered cats are likely to mark in and out of the home. It is a natural function of the territorial instinct, fueled by hormones. Some cats will even defecate to mark! I've had owners who complain about their cats defecating in the laundry basket or atop the bed; disgusting, yes, but common, especially if a new person has moved in. His or her strange smell and presence motivates the cat to cover the "interloper's" scent with feces or urine.

If your unneutered cat is marking, get her to the veterinarian and have it done! Often just doing so will stop the behavior. Whether she is or isn't neutered, be sure to clean the affected area well with an odor-neutralizing cleaner. If you see her about to mark, spray her with a plant sprayer bottle while saying "*No!*" If she targets one specific spot in the home, consider using a cat repellent spray on the area, a sprinkle of pepper, or even a few strips of double-sided tape.

If she still marks, restrict her to one or two rooms for a day or two; put her litter box in there with her, and feed her at exact times instead of free-feeding, as this will help you better predict when she has to elimi-nate. Once she can go a few days without marking, release her.

Lastly, if she begins to mark after moving into a new home, consider the possibility that the old carpets in the new home may smell of pre-vious pets. Clean or replace them!

Jumping Up

Cats are acrobats, and can leap up onto nearly any surface, no matter how high. Counters, tables, bookcases, and even the tops of open doors are all within a healthy cat's range. You may not mind this, but if you do, you'll need to take preventive measures, and start some boundary training. Here's how:

- **Never leave food out on tables or counters. Wipe everything down with a soapy sponge; the bitter taste will discourage her in the future.**

- **Keep plant sprayer bottles handy while eating, cooking or working at your desk. If she jumps up, give her a spray and say "*Off!*"**

- **Place strips of aluminum foil or double-sided tape on coun-ters, or wherever you want to her stay off of.**

Destructive Behavior

Though not as destructive as dogs, cats too can make a mess. Ripped furniture, torn carpets or pillows, chewed sweaters—almost anything can fall victim to a dedicated destroyer.

Many cats who destroy things are young and spirited, and just learning the ropes, while some are unneutered tyrants. Others, stressed out by something, are showing "displacement behavior": a way of releasing pent-up frustrations. Still others are simply bored and under-stimulated.

First, be sure your cat is neutered. Next, determine if it is marking behavior. Is she using the sofa as a scratching post? If so, purchase two new scratching posts of at least thirty inches in height, and place them near the sofa, while treating the sofa with a cat repellent spray. Next, study her home environment; is it stimulating, or boring? Study Secret Five, Enrich Your Cat's Environment, and apply any enrichment activities you deem appropriate. With more to do, she will have less reason to destroy.

Be sure she is healthy, as destructive behavior can be a symptom of illness or injury. She has no way to tell you where it hurts; acting out may be the only way for her to make her point.

Lastly, be sure to cat-proof the home. Keep clothing, pillows, wallets or anything she likes to damage out of sight!

Excess Vocalizing

Some cats are as quiet as the mice they crave, while others vocalize from morning to night. Part of this behavior can be breed-related; some breeds such as the Siamese or Burmese are natural chatterboxes, while the Persian or Scottish Fold tend to be a bit quieter. But all cats will vocalize according to their moods, needs or levels of perceived safety.

Cats will purr, meow, chirp, hiss, yowl, scream, growl—whatever they feel is appropriate at the time. Usually it is quite tolerable, and even pleasant for an owner. But sometimes it can get out of hand. For instance, a cat that is injured or under the weather might have no other way to communicate this to her owner other than vocally. If your normally quiet cat becomes noisy and nervous, think about getting her to her veterinarian for a checkup, as she could be ill.

Older cats can become more vocal because of a loss of hearing, something that happens naturally to people and pets later in life. Used to the normal sounds of the home, when your cat can no longer hear you, others in the home, or the typical auditory cues she has been used to her entire life, stress can build, causing the excess nervous vocalizations. If you have an older cat who suddenly starts talking it up, have her hearing checked.

Another cause of excess vocalizing can be the longing to mate. If you have an unneutered male or female, odds are the cat will start caterwauling and complaining whenever nature calls. For a female, that means whenever she comes into heat; for a male, it means whenever a female in heat wanders by the home. You can minimize your own cat's sex-related vocalizations through neutering.

Cat fights are particularly noisy. If you allow your cat outdoors, sooner or later she will get into a fight with another cat. The ensuing rumble will be loud and dramatic, and potentially damaging to your cat. To avoid this, *keep your cat indoors!*

Stress can cause an otherwise healthy cat to vocalize. If your cat checks out as healthy, odds are something in her environment might be the culprit. Examine the home; have you changed anything? Did someone leave, or has a new person or pet appeared? Did you recently kick her out of the bedroom? Redecorate? It could be anything; try to put your cat hat on and examine the situation. Even a change in food or litter can do it. Ordinarily her vocalizations will calm down over time, unless the issue is particularly upsetting to her, like a favorite cat buddy passing on. You can try to distract her with new toys and distractions; avoid getting a new pet, though, as this can make matters worse.

Curtain Climbing

Some crazy cats like to climb the curtains. What can I say; they are free spirits. Why do they do it? Several reasons: First, kittens and young cats are rambunctious, and simply want to play. Plus, the added benefit of getting up high adds to the fun. Or, a cat might simply be bored to tears in a home devoid of distractions, or wish to sit on a windowsill to enjoy watching the activity outside or sleep there in the sun. Whatever the reason, draperies can be torn by a climbing cat, making it an expensive problem for the owner.

You can try several tactics. First, consider going to a shorter style of curtain that ends mid-wall or just below the windowsill. Or, sweep the full-length curtains to the side and tie with a sash, or simply knot them, to make them less accessible. If your cat simply wants to reach the sill, perhaps she can then make the jump up, or you can arrange some other access.

Otherwise, another trick is to temporarily place strips of aluminum foil beneath the curtains. She will hate to walk on this, and as a result will not be able to get a decent "launch" platform from which to jump up. You can also try double-sided tape, if it will stick to the available flooring. If she *still* tries to climb, spray her with a plant sprayer bottle each time you catch her in the act.

A more stern solution (for the most stubborn cat) is to lift the curtain rod out of its holder, so that it is just balanced *atop* the brackets instead of snapped *into* them. When your cat jumps up onto the curtains, she will pull the entire unit down with her own weight. She won't get hurt, but she'll most likely never try the climbing act again!

Predatory Problems

Cats allowed outdoors will often bring back little trophies for you to see and share in. Though a natural behavior for a predator, the impact on the local animal population can be severe. Young birds can fall victim, especially when just learning to fly. Rodents, though not particularly pleasing to us, also have a place in the local ecosystem (unless they get inside your home).

Your local ecosystem and the animals within never planned on having thousands of skilled feline hunters roaming the territory; not indigenous to the food chain, cats can wreak havoc on some prey animals. And though it is flattering to have your cat bring you a half-dead sparrow, I am sure you'd rather be hearing the bird instead of seeing it. To that end, how about keeping your cat indoors? If not, at least attach a bell to her collar, to give the little prey animals a fighting chance.

Hiding

Timid cats often disappear for hours when guests arrive, or when anything out of the ordinary happens. Though not necessarily a normal behavior, cats have been for millions of years cautious creatures, able to hide themselves away from dangers in order to survive. If your cat hides whenever strangers arrive, she is simply employing this survival tactic, because she thinks it is needed.

Rescue cats, strays and abused cats are more apt to exhibit this behavior than are cats raised from kittenhood. They learn caution as a survival tool, and aren't about to abandon it that quickly. Shyer breeds like the Persian are also more likely to hide, as are longhaired breeds.

This behavior is hard to modify, as it goes deep into the cat's survival instincts. All you can do is to convince the cat over time that no actual threat exists. Often shy cats do come out of their hiding places to investigate; if yours does, quietly praise her, and let the visitor toss a treat or two onto the floor. Have the visitor remain passive, letting the cat decide on the level of contact she wants. Praise and reward when she shows up, and never force contact by picking her up and plopping her down into the guest's lap, a sure way to guarantee fear aggression.

Another technique you can use is to put your hiding cat on a regular feeding schedule, to better focus the food drive. Once you do this, treat offerings will have a bigger effect on her. You will then be able to lure her out of hiding, particularly near feeding time. You can even have a regular visitor prepare your cat's dinner and serve it to her a few times each week; though she may not actually appear at serving time, she will eventually begin to associate the smell of the stranger with the food, desensitizing her to the fear. You can even ring a bell at feeding time, to condition her that the sound means good things. Eventually you can ring the same bell when a guest comes over, then have the guest toss a treat on the floor.

Remember that shyness is not in and of itself a bad thing; if your cat is by nature a shrinking violet, don't take it personally. Simply let her determine her own comfort levels. Never force contact!

Roaming

Cats are territorial, and as such will want to establish their "turf." Though not as far ranging as dogs, cats are very covetous of their established territories, and will fight if need be to defend it.

Outdoor cats will typically roam up to several blocks away from home in an effort to define a territory. Anything inside this envelope is their hunting and mating province; other cats will be unwelcome, unless temporarily there to mate. The larger and more dominant a cat is the bigger and more well-guarded a territory will be; a big unneutered tomcat will have a bigger "spread" than will a small neutered female, and so on.

Though a normal feline behavior, roaming can result in injury or death from vehicles, and in unwanted pregnancy, illness, or death from infectious disease or parasitic infection. Or, your roaming cat can become a lost or "re-homed" cat. Roamers also get picked up by animal control officers, who bring the cats into municipal shelters, where the cat will normally be euthanized if not adopted out within a short span of time. Additionally, roaming cats become less socialized and more cautious, and become a burden on the small animal population.

The first step in alleviating this problem is to (you guessed it) never begin it. Keep your kittens indoors! By making your home a fun place to be with toys and other enrichments, you'll ensure a happier, safer cat. Next, neuter before sexual maturity, to curb the instinct to roam. For adopted cats used to going outdoors, consider a screened-in porch or deck, or a small fenced cat run accessible through a door or window. Many pet stores now sell pre-fabricated cat runs that assemble in minutes. You can even fence in your back yard with a secure, six-foot fence, then install a foot or so of overhanging "cat netting" atop it, leaning in toward the yard at an acute angle, preventing your cat from climbing out.

Fabric Chewing

Many cats love to chew or suck on fabric, especially wool or wool-type blends. Kittens or cats weaned too early sometimes develop this habit, particularly with clothing worn by their owners. Though a cute behavior, it can cost you a bundle, especially if the item in question is a cashmere sweater.

To stop the behavior, first be sure to closet all valuable clothing! Never leave clothing out, and keep your cat away from the laundry basket. Next, supply your cat with a few soft stuffed animals with the same texture. Sleep with them a few times to get your scent deep into them, then place them down in the living room. Be sure to regularly "recharge" them with your scent by rubbing them on you, or by putting them in the dirty laundry for a few hours.

If the behavior persists, try this: soak an old sweater in soapy water, dry without rinsing, then leave it out for the cat to suck on. When she does she'll get a mouthful of bitter soap. Or, spray the sweater with a cat repellent from the pet store. She should eventually get the message.

Finicky Eating

Some cats seem to barely pick at their food throughout the day, perhaps eating a few bits here and there, but never really appearing to eat heartily. Unlike dogs, who seem to gobble up everything in sight, most cats eat more selectively and slowly. This causes the owners of finicky cats to leave food down for the whole day, in order to placate their discriminating felines.

Cats prefer eating smaller portions of food on a more frequent basis. This may cause your cat to appear to be a finicky eater. Look closer, though, and you will see that the food does disappear, albeit at a slower pace.

Some cats get spoiled by owners who feed them tidbits of human food throughout the day. When presented with a dish of kibble for dinner, most cats will look up at you as if you were daft. The result: a cat who will only eat human leftovers.

If your cat normally eats well but has just recently begun shunning food, take him to your veterinarian for a checkup, as sudden changes in appetite can point to illness or injury.

The biggest cause of finicky eating in a cat is free-feeding, or leaving food down all day. Most owners use this method of feeding, replenishing food as the cat nibbles away at it. This procedure encourages your cat to eat only very small amounts of food on an almost continuous basis throughout the day, giving her the appearance of being finicky. The food is *always* there; why should she get worked up over it?

The best way to feed your finicky cat is to establish exact feeding times twice each day, and make food available to her for a short window of time, say forty-five minutes or so. Put the cat's dish down with whatever food you decide to feed her, while simultaneously ringing a bell or calling her name. If she comes and eats, so be it. If not, pick the food up. Then, later on in the day, repeat the procedure. If she eats, she eats. If not, remove the food. Eventually she will become hungry enough to get the picture.

In all likelihood this method will get your cat to pick up her appetite nicely. Do not let it go for more than a day or two, however, as cats can become very ill after a few days of not eating.

Avoid feeding your cat human food, as this will put her off of her normal food. Limit treats as well, especially with an over-finicky or obese cat. Consider feeding a quality canned food or even a raw diet, or at least mixing some canned into the cat's dry kibble. Canned or raw food is usually tastier and more palatable, and will often lure a finicky cat to the dinner dish.

Kneading

A common behavior with kittens still nursing, the kneading action is thought to help stimulate milk production in the mother. Often cats will carry this behavior over into adulthood, especially among those acquired at a very young age.

Normally this endearing behavior has no real down side to it; it's just a cute holdover from infancy. The only time it becomes a problem is when the cat in question begins to extend her claws while kneading, which can hurt exposed skin.

To avoid this, first consider either trimming your cat's nails yourself, or having the groomer or veterinarian do it for you. Keeping your cat's nails at a reasonable length will greatly reduce the chance of getting scratched during kneading. To learn how to do this yourself, refer to the Nails section in Secret Six.

Try wearing more protection when holding your cat in your lap. A long-sleeved shirt and long pants can all but alleviate painful scratches.

Noise Phobias

Most cats righteously abhor earsplitting noises such as thunder, airplanes, fireworks or raucous motorcycles. But some cats are intensely disturbed by loud sounds; even music, clapping, or loud laughter can set some cats running for the hills. In serious cases, some cats can even lose their housetraining, or attack someone in a fit of redirected aggression.

Timid, nervous cats tend to have a lower threshold of tolerance than do more confident cats. When these cats go into panic mode due to a sudden noise, they can disappear for hours, or run right up someone's leg in terror. I have even seen a terrified cat shoot up a curtain and hang upside down for half an hour, waiting for the smoke detector to stop screaming.

Prevention is the best medicine. If you know you have a timid cat, do your best to avoid loud noises, including music, fireworks, loud cars, or even hammering. Ask your family to respect her fears, and to not yell and scream indiscriminately around the home. This goes especially for small children, who can be a bit rambunctious from time to time. If there is construction or noisy traffic outdoors, keep windows and doors closed.

In the meantime, you can try to desensitize your cat to loud sounds. Begin by playing some pleasant music on the radio at a normal volume; slowly turn up the volume, so that after a few days of randomly playing music at increasing volume, she will tolerate it without fuss. You can also try clapping in her presence, followed by a treat reward. Increase the clap volume over a few days time until she does not freak out. You can try singing, snapping, or even tapping your foot; whatever she will tolerate. Through this, always reward her with treats and praise.

Conclusion

A Window into the Wild

Farther and farther removed from nature, we humans marvel at the cat's easy ability to maintain furtive links to both us and the untamed world. For this and many other reasons, we love them, and want to be near them.

The cat has never really been fully domesticated; rather I feel she has just been content to "visit" with us for the past few thousand years on an extended holiday of sorts. They love us, have no doubt; we are their silly siblings who, blessed with an abundance of food and comfort, make wonderful roommates and confidants. But if humanity ever did disappear, the cat would simply step back into the wild, without the need to alter her persona all that much.

The cat is slowly becoming not only the pet of choice for millions, but also a symbol for our increasingly independent culture. As society becomes less "pack-oriented" and more individualized, our pet preferences seem to evolve accordingly, favoring an animal who reflects a more self-reliant mindset. Cats are easier to maintain, less emotionally demanding, and come housebroken from the factory. And at a time when most feel an impersonal detachment from nature, cats manage to give some of it back to us with just a look, a whisk of a tail, or a gently running purr we can feel deep down.

Summary of the Seven Secrets

Abiding by the Seven Secrets is the best way to experience what your cat is all about. Let's revisit them one more time:

Secret One: Know Your Cat

Cats vary not only in appearance, but in behavior as well. Try to learn as much as you can about your breed or breed mix, to be prepared for whatever breed-specific behaviors might pop up. Also, the more you know about your cat's history the better, as it will help you better understand your cat's unique personality. The more you know about her, the easier it will be to create the optimal environment, and the most congenial relationship. If acquiring a new cat, be sure to choose one best suited to your expectations and home environment.

Secret Two: Embrace a Feline Attitude and Awareness

To be in harmony with your cat, develop what I call "effective feline empathy." You'll learn to *"be the cat,"* and connect on a deeper level. Be aware of her sensory abilities, her physical prowess and her instinctive drives, as well as the need to let her set the tone of the relationship.

Secret Three: Create a Parental Partnership

To properly manage your cat's behavior, foster what I call a "perpetual state of parenthood" with her. By becoming a "mother figure" in her eyes, you'll prevent undesirable behaviors, and ensure a respectful, loving relationship.

Secret Four: Educate Your Cat

Natural cat owners know that a smart cat is a happy cat. The more she understands, the more self-assured she will be. By increasing her vocabulary, teaching her a trick or two and gently exposing her to new stimuli, you'll boost her confidence, decrease boredom and improve the quality of your relationship.

Secret Five: Enrich Your Cat's Environment

Bored cats often evidence their boredom through misbehavior. By creating a stimulating home environment for your cat, you'll head bad behaviors off at the pass. Natural cat owners ensure their cat's happiness and good behavior by creating diverse, fun enrichment activities that their cats can enjoy anytime, day or night. By appealing to your cat's inquisitive nature, you'll improve home life for everyone.

Secret Six: Keep Your Cat Healthy and Safe

Natural cat owners make sure their cats are healthy, and secured from danger. A great diet, regular exercise and grooming, and annual veterinary visits, combined with a safe, "cat-proofed" home and caring supervision will guarantee long life and happiness for your kitty.

Secret Seven: Respect the Status Quo

Inconsistent, unpredictable home conditions can cause insecurity and misbehavior in most cats. Establishing a comfortable routine and then sticking to it will help minimize stress and misbehavior and foster confidence, essential for cat happiness.

Following these Seven Secrets in interacting and coping with the feline species will help avoid many problems and keep misunderstandings to a minimum. In time of uncertainty, remember:

BE THE CAT

Index

About the Author

Pet behaviorist and native New Yorker **Steve Duno** has trained thousands of animals. His fifteen books and innumerable Web and magazine articles have covered a wide variety of topics including breed profiling, obedience training, pet diet and health care, solutions for aggression and other problem behaviors, and even trick training for both dogs and cats. A former teacher, Steve has also written fiction, and even two golf books (in his spare time). His books have garnered him a number of appearances on television and radio.

Steve Duno lives in Seattle with his family, his ditsy shepard mix Flavio, and his über mutt Rico.